WORLD FAMOUS
SAS AND ELITE FORCES

WORLD FAMOUS
SAS AND
ELITE FORCES

Edited by Jon E. Lewis

This edition published and distributed by
Parragon Book Service Ltd, Bristol 1996

Produced by Magpie Books, 1996
First published 1994 by Magpie Books
an imprint of Robinson Publishing, London
Copyright © 1994 Robinson Publishing
Illustrations courtesy of Popperfoto

British Library Cataloguing-in-Publication Data
A catalogue record for this book is available
from the British Library

ISBN 0 75251 774 0
10 9 8 7 6 5 4 3 2 1

Printed and bound in the E.C.

Contents

Acknowledgements

Introductory material copyright © John E. Lewis

The editor has made every effort to locate all persons having any rights in the selections which appear in this volume and to secure permission from the holders of such rights. Any queries regarding the use of material should be addressed to the editor c/o the publishers.

"The Mussolini Rescue" is an extract from *My Life* by Otto Skorzeny.

"Wireless Ridge" is an extract from *2 Para Falklands* by Major-General John Frost. Copyright © John Frost 1983. Reprinted by permission of Ashford, Buchan and Enright.

"The Stand at Imjin River" is from *Cap of Honour* by David Scott Daniel, with A. H. Farrar-Hockley and E. L. T. Capel. Published by White Lion Publishers.

"Siege at Princes Gate" by Jon E. Lewis. Copyright © 1993 the author.

"The Eagles of Bastogne" is from *Four Stars of Hell* by Laurence Critchell. Copyright © 1947 Laurence Critchell. Published by Farrar, Strauss and Cudahy, Inc., NYC.

"The Scud Hunters" is copyright © John Amos (pseud. Jon E. Lewis).

"Birth of a Legend" is copyright © 1995 Jon E. Lewis.

Chapter One

THE MUSSOLINI RESCUE

Otto Skorzeny

O tto Skorzeny was a junior Waffen SS officer serving in Berlin when a chance decision resulted in his overnight appointment as Chief of Germany's Special Troops. Prompted by the success of the raid on St Nazaire by British Commandos, Hitler ordered the setting up of a German equivalent. The Army High Command, however, regarded the order as another Hitler whim, and pushed it around departmental pending trays. Eventually, it landed up on the desk of someone who remembered a university acquaintance who might do as leader of the new unit. And so Otto Skorzeny found himself plucked from behind a desk and brevetted Chief of Special Troops. To mark the occasion he was promoted — to the rank of Captain.

As the world was soon to discover, the German army had inadvertently appointed a man who not only believed in the commando concept, but had the ability to carry it out. Born in Austria in 1908, Skorzeny was physically imposing (six-foot four, with a duelling scar from ear to chin), charismatic, and daring. Within six months of his appointment, Skorzeny had not only welded together a commando force, but had brought off the most improbable exploit of the war — the rescue of the Italian dictator, Mussolini, in September 1943 from the mountain prison where he was held by Italian forces intent on surrender to the Allies.

Other dazzling adventures quickly followed. In September 1944 Skorzeny kidnapped the son of the Hungarian Regent and occupied the Citadel of Budapest (a move which prevented

Hungary concluding a separate peace with the USSR, and rescued a million encircled German troops). During the Ardennes Offensive, December 1944, he organized "American Brigades" of disguised Germans to cause havoc behind Allied lines. Eisenhower was a prisoner in his own HQ for a week.

With the conclusion of the war in Europe, Skorzeny (now a Major-General) was declared by the Allied Prosecutor to be "the most dangerous man in Europe", and charged with war crimes. The most serious of these related to "fighting in enemy uniform" during the Ardennes Offensive.

At one stage it looked as though Skorzeny would hang. This fate, however, was averted when his defence lawyer called as a witness the British war hero, Wing Commander Forrest Yeo-Thomas, who revealed that the British had done the same thing in reverse as a matter of course. Skorzeny was duly acquitted.

On his release from POW camp he settled in Spain, where he returned to his pre-war occupation of engineering. One of the most influential pioneers of special forces, Skorzeny died in 1975.

The following is Skorzeny's own account of his greatest triumph, the liberation of Mussolini from Gran Sasso, a mountain range to the north of Rome.

September 10th, 1943. We had not been out of our uniforms for two nights and days, and though our general was in the same case it was essential that I should see him with a view to making the great decision.

But first I discussed all the possibilities with Radl. We both fully realized that speed was absolutely vital. Every day, every hour that we delayed increased the danger that the Duce might be removed elsewhere, nay even worse, delivered over to the Allies. This supposition subsequently turned out to be most realistic. One of the terms of the armistice agreed by General Eisenhower was that the Duce should be handed over.

A ground operation seemed hopeless from the start. An attack on the steep, rocky slopes would have cost us heavy losses, as well as giving good notice to the enemy and leaving them time to conceal their prisoner. To forestall that eventuality, the whole massif would have to be surrounded by good mountain troops. A division at least would be required. So a ground operation was ruled out.

The factor of surprise could be our only trump as it was to be feared that the prisoner's guards had orders to kill him if there was any danger of rescue. This supposition later proved well founded. Such an order could only be frustrated by lightning intervention.

There remained only two alternatives – parachute landings or gliders.

We pondered long over both and then decided in favour of the second. At such altitudes, and in the thin air, a parachute drop would involve too rapid a rate of descent for anyone equipped with the normal parachute only. We also feared that in this rocky region the parachutists would be scattered too widely, so that an immediate attack by a compact detachment would not be possible.

So a glider remained the only solution. The final decision was in the hands of the Parachute Corps experts and General Student.

What were the prospects of success with glider landings? When we took our air photographs to the big laboratory at Frascati on the afternoon of the 8th, we had found it completely destroyed. I asked one of my officers to look somewhere else and he eventually found an emergency laboratory at an airstrip. Unfortunately, we could not have the usual big stereos which would have shown up all the details of the mountain zone. We would have to be content with ordinary prints approximately 14 by 14 cm.

These proved good enough to enable me to recognize the triangular meadow which I had noticed as we flew over. On the suitability of this meadow as a landing-ground we based our whole plan and I accordingly drew up detailed orders for the individual parties.

General Student suggested that a parachute battalion infiltrate by night into the valley and seize the lower station of the funicular at the hour appointed for the landing. In that way we should have cover on that side and also a line of retreat if withdrawal became necessary after the operation was complete.

The talk with General Student had the desired result. Of course he realized that there were many most serious objections but he agreed that there was only one possible way short of abandoning the enterprise altogether. Then the experts in air landings — the Chief-of-Staff and the Ia Air of the Parachute Corps — were called in to give their reactions.

These two officers were at first wholly adverse to the plan. They objected that an air landing of this kind at such an altitude and without a prepared landing-ground had never been attempted before. In their view the projected operation would result in the loss of at least 80 per cent of the troops employed. The survivors would be too few to have any chance of success.

My answer was that I was fully aware of this danger, but every novel venture must have a beginning. We knew the meadow was flat and a careful landing should enable us to avoid serious casualties. "Of course, gentlemen, I am ready to carry out any alternative scheme you may suggest."

After careful consideration, General Student gave his final approval and issued his orders: "The twelve gliders required are to be flown from the south of France to Rome at once. I fix 6 a.m. on September 12th as zero-hour. At that moment the machines must land on the plateau and the funicular station be seized by our battalion. We can assume that at that early hour the dangerous air currents so common in Italian mountain regions will be relatively weak. I will instruct the pilots personally and impress upon them the importance of the utmost care in landing. I am sure you are right, Captain Skorzeny. The operation cannot be carried out in any other way!"

SAS: THE HARDEST DAY

In July 1972 nine men of the British SAS were attacked by 250 communist guerillas at Mirbat, in the Sultanate of Oman. Completely surrounded, the fortified base (the 'Batthouse') of the SAS was subjected to withering fire by 75mm recoilless rifles, mortars, heavy machine guns and even a Carl Gustav 84mm rocket launcher. Though the SAS commanding officer, Mike Kealy, had never been in action before, he, along with Corporal Bradshaw, organized a devastating pattern and rate of return fire which chopped away at the advance of the guerillas. At one stage, though, the guerillas were so close that the SAS mortarman had to support the mortar barrel with his legs in a near-upright position. Several SAS men, including Kealy, made dashes amid the bullets to a nearby gunpit, to operate a 25 pounder belonging to the Sultan's gendarmerie. While Kealy was in the gunpit a grenade rolled in – but failed to explode. Minutes later Strikemaster jets of the Sultan's Air Force screamed in at low level, cannons firing, and the guerillas began to withdraw. The siege was over. For the loss of two men, the SAS had survived its hardest test.

After this decision had been given Radl and I worked out the details of our plan. We had to make careful calculations of the distances, make up our minds as to what arms and equipment the men should carry and, above all, prepare a large-scale plan showing the exact landing-place for each of the twelve gliders. Each glider could take ten men, i.e., a group, in addition to the pilot. Each group must know exactly what it had to do. I decided that I would go myself in the third glider so that the immediate assault by my own and the fourth group could be covered by the two groups already landed.

At the conclusion of these labours we spent a little time discussing our chances. We did not bluff ourselves that they were other than very slim. No one could really say whether Mussolini was still on the mountain and would not be spirited away elsewhere before we arrived. There was the further question whether we could overpower the guards quickly enough to prevent anyone killing him first, and we had not forgotten the warning given by the staff officers.

We must, in any event, allow for casualties in the landings. Even without any casualties we should only be 108 men and they could not all be available at the same moment. They would have to tackle 150 Italians who knew the ground perfectly and could use the hotel as a fortress. In weapons the two opponents could be regarded as approximately equals, as our parachutists' tommy-guns gave us an advantage, compensating to some extent for the enemy's superiority in numbers, particularly if we had not suffered too badly at the outset.

While we were immersed in these calculations Radl interrupted: "May I suggest, sir, that we forget all about figures and trying to compute our chances; we both know that they are very small, but we also know that, however small, we shall stake our lives on success!"

One more thought occurred to me: how could we increase the effect of surprise, obviously our most potent weapon? We racked our brains for a long time and then Radl suddenly had a bright idea: "Why not take with us an Italian officer, someone who must be reasonably well known to the Carabinieri up there? His very presence will bluff the guards for a short time and restrain them from immediately reacting to our arrival by violence against the Duce. We must make the best possible use of the interval."

This was an excellent idea, which I promptly approved and considered how best to exploit. General Student must confer with the officer in question during the evening before the operation and somehow persuade him to come with us. To prevent leakage or betrayal, he must remain with us until the following morning.

We discussed the choice of the most suitable person with someone who knew the situation in Rome and decided upon some high-ranking officer of the former Italian head-quarters in that city who had adopted a substantially neutral attitude during the recent disturbances. He must be invited to a conference at Frascati after General Student had approved the idea.

Fresh troubles now descended upon us. The reports we received during September 11th about the movement of the gliders were very unsatisfactory. Owing to enemy air activity they had had to make various detours and bad weather had not helped. Despite these misfortunes, we hoped to the last that they would arrive in time, but we hoped in vain.

The selected Italian officer, a general, appeared punctually, but had to be politely put off till the next day and invited to a conference with General Student for 8 p.m. at the Practica di Mare airfield. Zero-hour had to be postponed, as we received news that the gliders could not arrive in Rome before the early hours of the 12th. General Student fixed it for 2 o'clock on the Sunday (September 12th) as we certainly could not wait another twenty-four hours. This postponement involved awkward changes in our plans and further prejudiced our chances. Owing to the air currents and local winds to be anticipated in the middle of the day the landing would be more dangerous, and the fact that the assault was to be made at 2 p.m. (i.e. in broad daylight) set a difficult task for the detachment operating in the valley. Various changes were necessary and had to be made with the utmost speed.

In the afternoon of the Saturday I visited the garden of a monastery in Frascati where my own men and the Mors battalion had pitched their tents. For this enterprise I meant to take volunteers only, and I had no intention of keeping them in the dark as to the dangers involved. I had them paraded and made a short speech: "The long waiting-time is over. We have an important job to do tomorrow. Adolf Hitler has ordered it personally. Serious losses must be anticipated and, unfortunately, cannot be avoided. I shall of course lead you and can promise you that I will do my utmost. If we all stick together the assault will and must succeed. Anyone prepared to volunteer take one step forward!"

It gave me the greatest pleasure to see that not one of my men wanted to be left behind. To my officers and von Berlepsch commanding the one parachute company, I left the disagreeable task of refusing some of them, as the party must not exceed 108 in all. I myself selected 18 of my Waffen SS men. A small special commando was chosen for the valley detachment and another for an operation to rescue the Duce's family. I remained at the camp a little longer and was delighted with the spirit and enthusiasm everywhere displayed.

At that moment we got a terrible shock from an Allied wireless message which came through. It was to the effect that the Duce had arrived as a prisoner in Africa on board an Italian man-of-war which had come from Spezia. When I recovered from the fright I took a map and compasses. As we knew the exact moment when part of the Italian fleet left Spezia I could easily calculate that even the fastest ship could not possibly have reached Africa so soon. The wireless message must, therefore, be a hoax. Was I not justified in regarding all news from enemy sources with the greatest suspicion ever after?

Sunday, September 12th, 1943. At 5 a.m. we marched in close order to the airfield. There we learned that the gliders were expected at 10 a.m.

I again inspected the equipment of my men, who were all wearing parachute uniform. Parachute rations for five days had been issued. I had arranged that several boxes of fruit should be sent up and we sat about, pleasantly idle, in the shade of the buildings and trees. There was an atmosphere of tension, of course, but we took care to prevent any manifestation of apprehension or nerves.

By 8 o'clock, the Italian officer had not showed up so I had to send Radl off to Rome, telling him that the man had to be produced, alive, in double quick time. The trusty Radl duly produced him, though he had the greatest difficulty in finding him in the city.

General Student had a short talk with him in my presence, Lieutenant Warger acting as interpreter. We told him of Adolf Hitler's request for his participation in the operation, with a view to minimizing the chance of bloodshed. The officer was greatly flattered by this personal request from the head of the German state and found it impossible to refuse. He agreed, thereby placing an important trump in our hands.

At about 11 o'clock the first gliders came in. The towing planes were quickly refuelled and the coupled aircraft drawn up in the order in which they were to start. General Student dismissed the men of Berlepsch's company and then my men.

The pilots and the twelve group commanders were summoned to an inner room, where General Student made a short speech in which he again laid great stress on the absolute necessity for a smooth landing. He categorically forbade crash landings, in view of the danger involved.

I gave the glider commanders detailed instructions and drew a sketch on a blackboard showing the exact landing-place of each craft, after which I cleared up all outstanding points with the commanders of each group and explained the tasks allotted to them. The men had decided on their password, something guaranteed to shift all obstacles. It was "Take it easy", and the battle cry remained the watchword of the SS commandos right up to the end of the war.

Flying times, altitudes, and distances were then discussed with the Ic (Intelligence officer) of the Parachute Corps, who had been on the photographic expedition with us. He was to take his place in the first towing plane as, apart from Radl and myself, he alone knew the appearance of the ground from the air. The flying time for the 100 kilometres to be covered would be approximately one hour, so it was essential that we should start at 1 o'clock prompt.

At 12.30, there was a sudden air-raid warning. Enemy bombers were reported and before long we were hearing bomb bursts quite near. We all took cover and I cursed at the prospect of the whole enterprise being knocked on the head at the last moment. Just when I was in the depths of despair, I heard Radl's voice behind me: "Take it easy!" and confidence returned in a flash. The raid ended just before 1 o'clock. We rushed out to the tarmac and noticed several craters, though our gliders were unharmed. The men raced out to their aircraft and I gave the order to emplane, inviting the Italian General to sit in front of me on the narrow board, which was all that was available in the cramped space into which we were packed like herrings. There was in fact hardly any room for our weapons. The General looked as if he were already regretting his decision and had already shown some hesitation in following me into the glider. But I felt it was too late to bother about his feelings. There was no time for that sort of thing!

I glanced at my watch. 1 o'clock! I gave the signal to start. The engines began to roar and we were soon gliding along the tarmac and then rising into the air. We were off.

We slowly gained altitude in wide circles and the procession of gliders set course towards the north-east. The weather seemed almost ideal for our purpose. Vast banks of white cloud hung lazily at about 3,000 metres. If they did not disperse we should reach our target practically unobserved and drop out of the sky before anyone realized we were there.

The interior of the glider was most unpleasantly hot and stuffy. I suddenly noticed that the corporal sitting behind me was being sick and that the general in front had turned as green as his uniform. Flying obviously did not suit him; he certainly was not enjoying himself. The pilot reported our position as best he could and I carefully followed his indications on my map, noting when we passed over Tivoli. From the inside of the glider we could see little of the country. The cellophane side-windows were too thick and the gaps in the fabric (of which there were many) too narrow to give us any view. The German glider, type DFS 230, comprised a few steel members covered with canvas. We were somewhat backward in this field, I reflected, thinking enviously of an elegant aluminium frame.

We thrust through a thick bank of clouds to reach the altitude of 3,500 metres which had been specified. For a short time we were in a dense grey world, seeing nothing of our surroundings, and then we emerged into bright sunshine, leaving the clouds below us. At that moment the pilot of our towing machine, a Hentschel, came through on the telephone to the commander of my glider: "Flights 1 and 2 no longer ahead of us! Who's to take over the lead now?"

This was bad news. What had happened to them? At that time I did not know that I also had only seven machines instead of nine behind me. Two had fallen foul of a couple of bomb craters at the very start. I had a message put through: "We'll take over the lead ourselves!"

I got out my knife and slashed right and left in the fabric to make a hole big enough to give us something of a view. I changed my mind about our old-fashioned glider. At least it was made of something we could cut!

My peephole was enough to let us get our bearings when the cloud permitted. We had to be very smart in picking up bridges, roads, river bends and other geographical features on our maps. Even so, we had to correct our course from time to time. Our excursion should not fail through going astray. I did not dwell on the thought that we should be without covering fire when we landed.

It was just short of zero-hour when I recognized the valley of Aquila below us and also the leading vehicles of our own formation hastening along it. It would clearly be at the right place at the right time, though it must certainly have had its troubles too. We must not fail it!

"Helmets on!" I shouted as the hotel, our destination, came in sight, and then: "Slip the tow-ropes!" My words were followed by a sudden silence, broken only by the sound of the wind rushing past. The pilot turned in a wide circle, searching the ground — as I was doing — for the flat meadow appointed as our landing-ground. But a further, and ghastly, surprise was in store for us. It was triangular all right, but so far from being flat it was a steep, a very steep hillside! It could even have been a ski-jump.

We were now much nearer the rocky plateau than when we were photographing it and the conformation of the ground was more fully revealed. It was easy to see that a landing on this "meadow" was out of the question. My pilot, Lieutenant Meyer, must also have realized that the situation was critical, as I caught him looking all round. I was faced with a ticklish decision. If I obeyed the express orders of my General I should abandon the operation and try to glide down to the valley. If I was not prepared to do so, the forbidden crash-landing was the only alternative.

It did not take me long to decide. I called out: "Crash landing! As near to the hotel as you can get!" The pilot, not hesitating for a second, tilted the starboard wing and down we came with a rush. I wondered for a moment whether the glider could take the strain in the thin air, but there was little time for speculation. With the wind shrieking in our ears we approached our target I saw Lieutenant Meyer release the parachute brake, and then followed a crash and the noise of shattering wood. I closed my eyes and stopped thinking. One last mighty heave, and we came to rest.

The bolt of the exit hatch had been wrenched away, the first man was out like a shot and I let myself fall sideways out of the glider, clutching my weapons. We were within 15 metres of the hotel! We were surrounded by jagged rocks of all sizes, which may have nearly smashed us up but had also acted as a brake so that we had taxied barely 20 metres. The parachute brake now folded up immediately behind the glider.

The first Italian sentry was standing on the edge of a slight rise at one corner of the hotel. He seemed lost in amazement. I had no time to bother about our Italian passenger, though I had noticed him falling out of the glider at my side, but rushed straight into the hotel. I was glad that I had given the order that no one must fire a shot before I did. It was essential that the surprise should be complete. I could hear my men panting behind me. I knew that they were the pick of the bunch and would stick to me like glue and ask no explanations.

We reached the hotel. All the surprised and shocked sentry required was a shout of "*mani in alto*" (hands up). Passing through an open door, we spotted an Italian soldier engaged in using a wireless set. A hasty kick sent his chair flying from under him and a few hearty blows from my machine-pistol wrecked his apparatus. On finding that the room had no exit into the interior of the hotel we hastily retraced our steps and went outside again.

We raced along the façade of the building and round the corner to find ourselves faced with a terrace 2.50 to 3 metres high. Corporal Himmel offered me his back and I was up and over in a trice. The others followed in a bunch.

13

My eyes swept the façade and lit on a well-known face at one of the windows of the first storey. It was the Duce! Now I knew that our effort had not been in vain! I yelled at him: "Away from the window!" and we rushed into the entrance hall, colliding with a lot of Italian soldiers pouring out. Two machine-guns were set up on the floor of the terrace. We jumped over them and put them out of action. The Carabinieri continued to stream out and it took a few far from gentle blows from my weapon to force a way through them. My men yelled out *"mani in alto"*. So far no one had fired a shot.

I was now well inside the hall. I could not look round or bother about what was happening behind me. On the right was a staircase. I leaped up it, three steps at a time, turned left along a corridor and flung open a door on the right. It was a happy choice. Mussolini and two Italian officers were standing in the middle of the room. I thrust them aside and made them stand with their backs to the door. In a moment my Untersturmführer Schwerdt appeared. He took the situation in at a glance and hustled the mightily surprised Italian officers out of the room and into the corridor. The door closed behind us.

We had succeeded in the first part of our venture. The Duce was safely in our hands. Not more than three or four minutes had passed since we arrived!

At that moment the heads of Holzer and Benz, two of my subordinates, appeared at the window. They had not been able to force their way through the crowd in the hall and so had been compelled to join me via the lightning-conductor. There was no question of my men leaving me in the lurch. I sent them to guard the corridor.

I went to the window and saw Radl and his SS men running towards the hotel. Behind them crawled Obersturmführer Merzel, the company commander of our Friedenthal special unit and in charge of glider 4 behind me. His glider had grounded about 100 metres from the hotel and he had broken his ankle on landing. The third group in glider 5 also arrived while I was watching.

I shouted out: "Everything's all right! Mount guard everywhere!"

I stayed a little while longer to watch gliders 6 and 7 crashland with Lieutenant Berlespsch and his parachute company. Then before my very eyes followed a tragedy. Glider 8 must have been caught in a gust; it wobbled and then fell like a stone, landed on a rocky slope and was smashed to smithereens.

Sounds of firing could now be heard in the distance and I put my head into the corridor and shouted for the officer-in-command at the hotel. A colonel appeared from nearby and I summoned him to surrender forthwith, assuring him that any further resistance was useless. He asked me for time to consider the matter. I gave him one minute, during which Radl turned up. He had had to fight his way through and I assumed that the Italians were still holding the entrance, as no one had joined me.

The Italian colonel returned, carrying a goblet of red wine which he proffered to me with a slight bow and the words: "To the victor!"

A white bedspread, hung from the window, performed the functions of a white flag.

After giving a few orders to my men outside the hotel I was able to devote attention to Mussolini, who was standing in a corner with Untersturmführer Schwerdt in front of him. I introduced myself: "Duce, the Führer has sent me! You are free!"

Mussolini embraced me: "I knew my friend Adolf Hitler would not leave me in the lurch," he said.

The surrender was speedily carried out. The Italian other ranks had to deposit their arms in the dining-room of the hotel but I allowed the officers to keep their revolvers. I learned that we had captured a general in addition to the colonel.

I was informed by telephone that the station of the funicular had also fallen undamaged into our hands. There had been little fighting, but the troops had arrived to the second and the surprise had been complete.

Lieutenant von Berlepsch had already replaced his monocle when I called to him from the window and gave orders that reinforcements must be sent up by the funicular. I wanted to make insurance doubly sure and also show the Italian colonel that we had troops in the valley also. I then had our wireless truck in the valley called up on the telephone with instructions to send out a message to General Student that the operation had succeeded.

The first to arrive by the funicular was Major Mors, commanding the parachute formation in the valley. Of course the inevitable journalist put in an appearance. He immediately made a film to immortalize the hotel, the damaged gliders and the actors in the drama. He made a mess of it and later on I was very annoyed that the pictures in the magazine suggested that he had himself taken part in the operation. We certainly had too much to do in the first moments to find time to pose for reporters.

Major Mors then asked me to present him to the Duce, a request I was very pleased to comply with.

I was now responsible for Mussolini and my first anxiety was how we were to get him to Rome. Our plan had provided for three possibilities.

Both he and I considered that it would be too dangerous to travel 150 kilometres by road through an area which had not been occupied by German troops since the defection of Italy. I had therefore agreed with General Student that Plan A should be the sudden *coup de main* against the Italian airfield of Aquila de Abruzzi, at the entrance to the valley. We should hold it only a short time. I would give the zero-hour for this attack by wireless and a few minutes later three German He 111s would land. One of them would pick up the Duce and myself and leave at once, while the two others gave us cover and drew off any aircraft pursuing.

Plan B provided that a Fieseler-Storch should land in one of the meadows adjoining the valley station. Plan C was for Captain Gerlach to attempt a landing with the Fieseler-Storch on the plateau itself.

Our wireless truck got through to Rome with the report of our success, but when I had fixed up a new time-table with Lieutenant Berlepsch and tried to give the parachutists the zero-hour, 4 o'clock, for the attack on the airfield we found we could not make contact. That was the end of Plan A.

I had watched the landing of one of the Fieseler-Storchs in the valley through my glasses. I at once used the telephone of the funicular to have the pilot instructed to prepare to take off again at once. The answer came back that the aircraft had suffered some damage on landing and could not be ready straight away. So only the last and most dangerous alternative, Plan C, remained.

After they had been disarmed, the Italian other ranks showed themselves extremely helpful and some of them had joined with the men we had sent out to rescue the victims of the glider crash. Through our glasses we had seen some of them moving, so that we could hope that it had not been fatal to all its occupants. Other Carabinieri now helped in clearing a small strip. The biggest boulders were hastily removed, while Captain Gerlach circled overhead and waited for the agreed signal to land. He proved himself a master in the art of emergency landing, but when I told him how we proposed to make a getaway with his help he was anything but pleased with the prospect, and when I added that there would be three of us he said bluntly that the idea was impracticable.

I had to take him aside for a short but tense discussion. The strength of my arguments convinced him at last. I had indeed considered every aspect of the matter most carefully and fully realized my heavy responsibility in joining the other two. But could I possibly justify letting the Duce go alone with Gerlach? If there was a disaster, all that was left for me was a bullet from my own revolver: Adolf Hitler would never forgive such an end to our venture. As there was no other way of getting the Duce safely to Rome it was better to share the danger with him, even though my presence added to it. If we failed, the same fate would overtake us all.

In this critical hour I did not fail to consult my trusty friend, Radl. I then discussed with him and Major Mors the question of how we were to get back. The only men we wanted to take with us were the general and the colonel, and we must get them to Rome as soon as possible. The Carabinieri and their officers could be left at the hotel. The Duce had told me that he had been properly treated, so that there was no reason not to be generous. My pleasure at our success was so great that I wanted to spare my opponents.

To guard against sabotage to the cable railway I ordered that two Italian officers should ride in each cage and that after we had got away the machinery should be damaged sufficiently to prevent its being put in working order again for some time. All other details I left to Major Mors.

Now at last, I had time to pay a little attention to the Duce. I had seen him once before, in 1943, when he was addressing the crowd from the balcony of the Palazzo Venezia. I must admit that the familiar photographs of him in full uniform bore little resemblance to the man in the ill-fitting and far from smart civilian suit who now stood before me. But there was no mistaking his striking features, though he struck me as having aged a lot. Actually he looked very ill, an impression intensified by the fact that he was unshaved and his usually smooth, powerful head was covered with short, stubbly hair. But the big, black, burning eyes were unmistakably those of the Italian dictator. They seemed to bore right into me as he talked on in his lively, southern fashion.

He gave me some intensely interesting details about his fall and imprisonment. In return I managed to give him some pleasant news: "We have also concerned ourselves with the fate of your family, Duce. Your wife and the two youngest children were interned by the new government in your country place at Bocca della Caminata. We got in touch with Donna Rachele some weeks ago. While we were landing here another of my commandos, under Hauptsturmführer Mandel, was sent to fetch your family. I'm sure they are free by now!"

The Duce shook my hand warmly. "So everything's all right. I'm very grateful to you!"

Donning a loose winter overcoat and a dark, soft hat, the Duce came out of the door. I went ahead to the waiting Storch. Mussolini took the rear seat and I stowed myself in behind. I noticed a slight hesitation before he climbed in and recollected that he was a pilot himself and could well appreciate the risks he was running.

The engine worked up to full speed and we nodded to the comrades we were leaving behind. I seized a stay in each hand and by moving my body up and down, tried to give the aircraft more thrust or lessen the weight. Gerlach signalled the men holding the wings and tail to let go and the airscrew drew us forward. I thought I heard a mixture of "Evviva"s and "Heil"s through the cellophane windows.

But, although our speed increased and we were rapidly approaching the end of the strip, we failed to rise. I swayed about madly and we had hopped over many a boulder when a yawning gully appeared right in our path. I was just thinking that this really was the end when our bird suddenly rose into the air. I breathed a silent prayer of thanksgiving!

Then the left landing-wheel hit the ground again, the machine tipped downwards and we made straight for the gully. Veering left, we shot over the edge. I closed my eyes, held my breath and again waited the inevitable end. The wind roared in our ears.

Mussolini talks with his rescuers from the cockpit, 16th October 1943

It must have been all over in a matter of seconds, for when I looked around again Gerlach had got the machine out of its dive and almost on a level keel. Now we had sufficient airspeed, even in this thin air. Flying barely 30 metres above the ground, we emerged in the Arrezzano valley.

All three of us were decidedly paler than we had been a few minutes earlier, but no words were wasted. In most unsoldierly fashion I laid my hand on the shoulder of Benito Mussolini whose rescue was now beyond doubt.

Having recovered his composure, he was soon telling me stories about the region through which we were flying at an altitude of 100 metres, carefully avoiding the hilltops. "Just here I addressed a huge crowd twenty years ago." . . . "Here's where we buried an old friend" . . . the Duce reminisced.

At length Rome lay below us, on our way to Practica di Mare. "Hold tight! Two-point landing," Gerlach shouted, reminding me of the damage to our landing-gear. Balancing on the right front and tail landing-wheels, we carefully touched down. Our trip was over.

Captain Melzer welcomed us in the name of General Student and congratulated us warmly on our success. Three He 111s were waiting for us, and after the conventions had been observed by my formally presenting their crews to the Duce, I gratefully shook Gerlach's hand on parting. There was no time to lose if we were to reach Vienna before dark.

Afterword

Hitler was ecstatic at the news of Mussolini's rescue, and danced for the first time since the Fall of France. He awarded Skorzeny the Knight's Cross personally.

Chapter Two

WIRELESS RIDGE

John Frost

T he British Army's Second Battalion of The Parachute
Regiment fought in all the major battles of the 1982 land
war between Britain and Argentina for the Falkland Islands
(Malvinas). After spearheading the landings at San Carlos on 21
May, the battalion fought its way to Port Stanley against
determined Argentinian resistance, via Bluff Cove, Goose Green
and Wireless Ridge. The most famous of these battles is
undoubtedly Goose Green (where 2 Para commander, Lieutenant-Colonel "H" Jones, won a posthumous Victoria Cross for
his charge against an enemy position), but the engagement at
Wireless Ridge on 13–14 June was no less dramatic. The Ridge, a
spur on the north side of Port Stanley, was heavily defended by
troops from the Argentine 7th Infantry Regiment and the
Argentine 1st Parachute Regiment. The story of the battle is
told here by Major-General John Frost, CB, DSO, MC, who
served with 2 Para in WWII, commanding the Battalion from
October 1942 until his capture at Arnhem, 1944, where he led
the defence of the bridge.

The origins of The Parachute Regiment lie with an initiative of
Winston Churchill who, after noting the success of German
paratroop operations during Germany's invasion of Holland and
Belgium, suggested the formation of a British airborne elite force.
The first units began training in June 1940, with volunteers from
the units forming The Parachute Regiment in August 1942.

Para's task was to capture the Wireless Ridge features,
keeping west of the telegraph wires, and Colonel Chaundler's plan called for a two-phase noisy night attack. In

Phase 1, A Company would take the northern spur where the ponds were, C Company having secured the start-line. Once this was secure Phase 2 would come into operation, and B and D Companies would pass through from the north to attack the main Wireless Ridge feature itself. B Company would go to the right (the western end of the ridge), while D Company attacked the rocky ridge-line east of the track.

The mortars would move forward from Mount Kent to a position in the lee of the hillside south of Drunken Rock Pass, and this would also be the site for a static Battalion Headquarters during the attack. H-hour was again to be at about 0030. The importance of digging in on the objectives was emphasized once more, since Wireless Ridge was dominated by both Tumbledown and Sapper Hill, and if enemy troops should still be there at dawn they could make 2 Para's positions untenable.

The orders were straightforward, and the plan simple, involving the maximum use of darkness. As the "O" Group ended the company commanders were told that they would now fly up to Mount Longdon to look at the ground over which they would operate.

The CO went on ahead with the Battery Commander to meet Lieutenant-Colonel Hew Pike, CO of 3 Para, and Major William McCracken, RA, who controlled the artillery "anchor" OP on Mount Longdon. They discussed and arranged for co-ordinated fire support, with 3 Para's mortars, Milan teams and machine-guns all ready to fire from the flank, and Major Martin Osborne's C Company, 3 Para, in reserve.

Back at the gully all was peaceful in the bright sunshine. Suddenly this was shattered as nine Skyhawks appeared further to the north, flying very low in formation and heading due west towards Mount Kent. The effect was electric, for no one expected that the Argentines could still flaunt their air power in this way.

At "A" Echelon, behind Mount Kent, there was no doubt as to who the jets were aiming for. As they came screaming up over the col and rose to attacking height, the formation split: three went for the area where the artillery gun-line had recently been, three went for 3 Commando Brigade HQ, and three attacked "A" Echelon. All the machine-guns opened up, claiming one possible hit as the bombs rained down. Amazingly, there were no casualties from this minor blitzkrieg. But the accuracy of the attack, and its obvious definiteness of purpose, left people wondering if the enemy had left concealed OPs behind, watching Mount Kent, or if satellite photography had shown up the various targets or, possibly, if Argentine electronic-warfare equipment had picked up radio signals from Brigade HQ.

The air raid created delays to all helicopter movement, but eventually the CO was able to fly on to Brigade HQ, while the company commanders were dropped on to Mount Longdon for their own recces. Colonel Chaundler had already been updated on the actual strength of the enemy, which was greater than had been thought, and a new Argentine position had been detected to the east of the pond-covered spur, on a knoll overlooking Hearnden Water and the mouth of the Murrell River.

While the CO was at Brigade HQ, the company commanders were able to study Wireless Ridge in detail from the commanding position on Longdon. It at once became obvious that much of the information so far given to them was inaccurate. What was thought to be C Company of 3 Para proved to be nothing of the sort: Major Dair Farrar-Hockley noticed that it was an *enemy* position of about company strength, situated dangerously on the flank of the 2 Para axis of attack, west of the northern spur. It was also clear that Wireless Ridge proper was heavily defended, with positions which stretched a long way to the east beyond the line of telegraph poles that marked the 2 Para boundary. Strangely, no harassing fire was being brought to bear during the day on any of the Argentine positions, and their soldiers were free to stand about in the open.

The company commanders flew back to Furze Bush Pass, but clearly a major change in plan was necessary. The CO returned from Brigade HQ as evening approached and was told of the situation. "Go away and have your supper. Come back in forty-five minutes and you will have a new set of orders," he said. Meanwhile the move-up of mortars and the adjustment of artillery had been delayed, and as a result the changes to the fireplan had to continue into the night, directed by the OP on Longdon and using illuminating rounds.

Unfortunately for the company commanders, normal battle procedure had already ensured that relevant details of the first plan had permeated to the lowest level. Platoon and section commanders had had time to issue clear and well constructed orders to their subordinates, but now their efforts were all useless, for by the time the company commanders returned with the CO's revised plan, it was too late to go into new details. Such a sudden last-minute change did little for the men's faith in the system, but it was unavoidable and, in any case, the soldiers had by now become stoical, while the cynics among them were not disappointed by this evidence of fallibility at higher levels. Nevertheless, the battalion was able to adapt and change its plans and moved off on time. But Phil Neame had his misgivings about what the SAS to the east of his line of advance was *meant* to be doing, and there was no knowledge of what the SAS was actually *going* to do. Furthermore, no one really knew what was beyond Wireless Ridge to the south, in the Moody Brook area, and everyone would have liked to have known exactly when the 5 Brigade attack on Tumbledown was timed to begin.

The battalion's new plan was for a four-phase noisy night attack. In Phase 1 D Company would capture the newly discovered enemy position west of the northern spur; A and B Companies would then assault the pond-covered hilltop; Phase 3 called for C Company to take the knoll to the east;

and finally D Company would roll up the enemy on Wireless Ridge itself, with fire support from A and B Companies, starting in the west and finishing at the telegraph poles.

Fire support was to be lavish in comparison to Goose Green: two batteries of 105-mm guns, HMS *Ambuscade* with her one 4.5-inch gun offshore, and the mortars of both 2 and 3 Para, totalling sixteen tubes. Ammunition was plentiful, and the battalion's mortars had been moved complete from Mount Kent by helicopter, and were thus fresh for action. The Machine-Gun Platoon had also been flown forward. Between the six guns they had enough ammunition to provide a massive weight of fire, and the men were fresh and rather proud of their earlier achievement behind Mount Kent against the Skyhawks. The Milan Platoon was already forward with the battalion — the experience of Goose Green had demonstrated the capability of this precision-guided missile against static defences. Finally the light tanks of the Blues and Royals would be there, Scimitars with their 30-mm automatic cannon and Scorpions with 76-mm guns, and both equipped with very high quality night-vision equipment and having superb cross-country performance. All available support was allotted first to D Company, then to A and B in their assault, and finally to D Company again as it traversed the ridge.

As night closed in the tanks, the mortars and the Recce Platoon, which was to secure the start-line, moved up. By now the promise of the day had vanished and snow and sleet were falling, considerably limiting the effectiveness of all the gunsighting equipment, and reducing visibility.

At about 0015 a storm of fire from the supporting artillery and mortars was unleashed upon the Argentine positions. A and B Companies passed by, led by C Company patrols to the new start-line secured by Corporal Bishop's patrol in the relatively safe ground overlooking

Lower Pass. At 0045 hours on Monday 14 June, D Company moved over its own start-line further to the west, and headed towards the identified enemy position.

As the company moved forward, the tanks of the Blues and Royals and the machine-guns provided fire support while the artillery increased its rate of fire. Enemy mortar fire in retaliation became heavy. In the rear of the company, Private Godfrey of 12 Platoon had a near miss as a piece of shrapnel cut through his windproof and dug into his boot. He dived for cover – straight into an Argentine latrine!

The weight of supporting artillery and mortar fire was singularly effective, for the enemy on the D Company objective could be seen running away as the company pushed forward, although 155-mm air-burst shelling increased as the Paras began to clear the Argentine trenches, now abandoned except for a few enemy killed by the barrage. The darkness of the night and the extent of the enemy position caused the company to spread out, creating problems of control. Lieutenant Webster of 10 Platoon counted up to twenty trenches on his right, with more over to the left, where 2nd Lieutenant Waddington's 11 Platoon found the other half of the assault formation.

Occasionally as they moved forward, men would suddenly disappear into the freezing water of an ice-covered pond. Privates Dean and Creasey of 11 Platoon went in up to their necks, and had to tread water to stay afloat until their platoon sergeant, Sergeant Light, dragged them out.

Fire support for the company was immaculate. The tanks used their powerful image-intensifier night-sights to pinpoint targets. Once enemy positions were identified, they fired. As soon as the battalion's machine-gunners saw the strike they, too, opened up. Occasionally the machine-gun fire was too close for comfort, even for D Company, and in the end 10 Platoon Commander called for it to stop.

The opposition had fled, and D Company took its first objective in record time, remaining *in situ* while A and B

Companies began their part of the battle. Enemy artillery fire was increasing, however, and Neame therefore decided to push forward for another 300 metres into relative safety, to avoid the worst of the barrage.

Several of those waiting to move on the A and B Company start-lines were reminded of scenes they had seen from films of the First and Second World Wars. As shells landed all around, men lay huddled against the peat, with bayonets fixed. There could be no denying that, for the soldiers, fear of the known was in this case worse than blissful ignorance of the unknown. In the shelter of the peat bogs some smoked, watching the display of illuminants above.

Just as the time came to move, the shelling claimed its first victim, for Colour Sergeant "Doc" Findlay was killed in the rear of A Company, and soldiers from Support and HQ Companies were also wounded. The advance began, the two companies moving southwards parallel to each other, on either side of the track. The men crossed the stream in the valley north of their objective with the tanks firing over their heads. The effect upon the enemy was devastating. In their night-sights the tank crews could see Argentine soldiers running or falling as the accurate fire took effect. The boost to morale that this form of suppressive fire gave was considerable; fundamentally, the battle was being won by supporting arms, the infantry being free to do their own job, which is actually clearing and securing the ground.

On the left, all was going well with A Company. Command and control had been well practised back at Goose Green and now the junior officers and section commanders were quite expert in maintaining direction. Silence was unnecessary and orders were shouted backwards and forwards. The enemy were still shelling as the companies advanced, but now counter-battery fire was being provided by our own artillery. From his own position the CO could see the two companies in extended formation, moving quickly up the hill, the whole battlefield brightly lit by starshell.

Co-ordinating the two assaulting companies' advances was difficult, however. The track provided a boundary of sorts, but controlling upwards of 200 men during a noisy battle over difficult terrain is not easy. Colonel Chaundler had another worry. Earlier, before the battalion had moved up, he had been shown a captured Argentine map which indicated a minefield directly in the path of the assaulting companies. There was only fifteen minutes to go before 2 Para set off — far too late for a change of plan. The CO only had time to brief OC B Company, while John Crosland had none in which to warn his men, and in any case was told to push on regardless, since there would be no time to clear the mines. Only afterwards did Major Crosland tell his men that they had actually moved directly through the minefield without knowing it. Miraculously, no one was blown up on the way.

The ponds on the spur claimed a victim, however, when Private Philpott of 5 Platoon suddenly plunged into over six feet of water. He was dragged out and his section commander, Corporal Curtis, immediately organized a complete change of clothing from the other men in the section, which probably saved Philpott's life.

The two companies consolidated on the objective. There was some firing from the trenches, swiftly silenced as the men of both companies ran in to clear them. Once more the enemy had fled, leaving only twenty or so of their number behind, quickly taken prisoner as they were winkled out of their holes. Radios were still switched on, and several dead lay around the positions. As the men dug in, the enemy shelling increased and it was to continue for the rest of the night at the same level of intensity. Most thought it was worse than Goose Green, but fortunately the abandoned enemy bunkers provided reasonable shelter, although a number of casualties occurred in A Company.

It was now C Company's turn. Already they had had a minor scare on the A and B Company start-line when a Scorpion tank had careered towards Company Headquarters in the darkness. It was hopelessly lost and its commander had to be evacuated after a dose of "hatch rash" — the effect of placing the head in the path of a rapidly closing hatch. The confused vehicle was soon heading in the right direction, but now under the command of Captain Roger Field, who had seized this opportunity to revert to a more honourable role than foot-slogging.

With A and B Companies now firm, C Company was ordered to check out the Argentine position further to the east that had been spotted from Mount Longdon on the previous day. Major Roger Jenner was glad to be moving again, for it seemed that the supporting artillery battery had developed a "rogue gun" and every sixth round meant for the enemy was coming in uncomfortably close to his company. He and his men set off, taking cover occasionally on the way as shells fell close by. There had been no firing from the company objective during the battle, and soon the platoons were pushing round the side of a minefield on to the knoll.

As the Recce Platoon advanced, they could hear noises of weapons being cocked. The bright moonlight left them uncomfortably exposed on the hillside. On the forward edge of the slope were two parallel lines of rock, and on the second line the platoon found a series of shell scrapes, suggesting recent occupation by a body of troops. Once again it seemed that the enemy had left hurriedly, leaving tents and bits of equipment behind in the process. Away over to the east Jenner's men could see the bright lights of Stanley airfield, and could hear a C-130 landing. The company was ordered to dig in, but since an enemy attack on this feature was extremely unlikely the CO changed the orders, and C Company moved up to the pond-covered hill.

If any particular group deserves special praise for what

was done that night, then it must be the tanks of the Blues and Royals. Their mere presence had been a remarkable boost to morale during all the attacks that had taken place, and the speed and accuracy of their fire, matched by their ability to keep up with the advancing Paras, had been a severe shock to the enemy. Lance-Corporal Dunkeley's tank, which Captain Field had taken over following the injury to its commander, had alone fired forty rounds from its 76-mm gun.

2 Para was performing superbly, its three first objectives taken with great speed and a minimum of casualties, despite heavy and accurate enemy artillery fire. Whenever the enemy in trenches had sought to return fire they had been met by a withering concentration of fire from the rifle companies' weapons which, coupled with very heavy support, had proved devastating. It is not known whether the Argentines had gathered that they were facing the men from Goose Green, but there can be no question that 2 Para knew.

D Company was now ready to go into the final phase of the attack and began moving forward again to the west end of Wireless Ridge. The tanks and support weapons moved up to join A and B Companies on the hilltop overlooking the D Company objective, and endured the artillery fire as well as anti-tank fire from Wireless Ridge to the south.

12 Platoon was now in the lead. Lieutenant John Page, who had taken over from the tragically killed Jim Barry, looked for the fence, running at right-angles to the ridge, that would guide him to the correct start-line for the assault. Unfortunately there was little left of the fence marked on the maps, and Corporal Barton's section, at the point of the platoon, could only find a few strands of wire to follow. The number of ice-covered ponds added to the difficulty and the intense cold was beginning to affect men's reactions, as they worked their way south to the western end of Wireless Ridge.

JAPANESE 201ST AIR GROUP: KAMIKAZE!
On the 25th October 1944 a Japanese Zero
aircraft screamed out of the sky above Leyte
Gulf, in the Phillipines. Sailors in the American
fleet below watched in paralysed horror as the
Zero, guns blazing, dived straight at the carrier
USS *Santee*, blowing an enormous hole in the
flight deck. The Japanese suicide pilots had made
their first attack. Dubbed 'Kamikaze', or Divine
Wind in reference to the typhoon which saved
Japan from invasion in the 13th Century, the
volunteer suicide pilots were a last desperate
gamble to halt the US tide in the Pacific
Theatre. The pilots, who were treated as gods
in Japan, drew for inspiration on the *Bushido*
code of the old Samurai warrior class, especially
its vaunting of the 'good death' in battle. Flying
aircraft loaded with 550lb bombs the Kamikaze
achieved spectacular successes, particularly after
the introduction of the *kikusui* ('floating
chrysanthemum'), which consisted of mass
attacks by suicide bombers. During the battle of
Okinawa, *kikusui* were responsible for the
sinking of 44 US vessels. Thereafter, to
American relief, Japan simply ran out of aircraft
to continue the kamikaze attacks.

Once more, massive fire-power began to soften up the
enemy, who apparently still had no intimation that they
were about to be rolled up from a flank. The initial idea had
been for D Company simply to sweep eastwards along the
ridge without stopping, with 11 Platoon on the left, 12
Platoon on the right and 10 Platoon in reserve. There was

still uncertainty as to whether Tumbledown to the south had been taken or not, and clearly a battle was still in progress on that mountain as the Scots Guards fought to drive out the Argentines on its summit. But Neame and his D Company had no intention other than to push on regardless, although they knew that if Tumbledown was still in enemy hands by daylight then 2 Para would be extremely vulnerable.

The bombardment of the western end of the Wireless Ridge continued as the platoons advanced. It seemed to have been effective, since no enemy were encountered at all, although, to be certain, 11 Platoon cleared any bunkers they came across on the reverse slope with grenades.

The first part of Wireless Ridge was now clear and across the dip, where the track came up, lay the narrower rocky outcrops of the remainder of the objective. Fire was concentrated on these areas from A and B Companies as tanks, Milans and machine-guns provided an intense concentration on to three enemy machine-gun posts that remained.

Efforts to switch artillery support further forward and on to the area of Moody Brook had unfortunate results. Five rounds of high explosive crashed on to the ridge around and very near the leading D Company platoons. 3 Section of 11 Platoon was caught in the open and, despite screams to stop the firing, it was too late. Private Parr was killed instantly, and Corporal McAuley was somersaulted into some rocks, completely dazed, and had to be picked up by a stretcher party.

There was a considerable delay while a livid Major Neame tried to get the gunners to sort themselves out. It seemed that one gun was off target, as C Company had noted, but at the gun-lines they did not know which, since in the dark it was impossible to note the fall of shot, even if there had been time, and the other battery was not available owing to shortage of ammunition. In the meantime the CO was growing increasingly impatient, urging the D Company commander to press on.

As soon as the gunners could guarantee reasonable support, and with increased efforts from the Blues and Royals, Neame was off again. All through the wait constant harassing fire from the enemy had been landing around the company, so none were sorry to move. Despite the fire pouring on to the ridge-line ahead, enemy machine-gunners continued firing from well sited bunkers, and were still staunchly in action as the platoons advanced.

They moved with 11 Platoon on the left, 12 Platoon ahead on the ridge itself, with the company commander immediately behind and, in the rear, 10 Platoon. 12 Platoon came across an abandoned Argentine recoilless rifle, an anti-tank weapon, as they crossed the start-line, which may well have been the weapon that had earlier been engaging the tanks on the A and B Company positions. The platoon moved down into the gap between the two parts of the ridge line, but as the soldiers passed by some ponds, very heavy machine-gun fire began from their front and illumination was called for as the platoon answered the firing. Corporal Barton came across some orange string, possibly indicating a minefield, but his platoon commander urged him on regardless.

The enemy appeared to be surprised by the direction of the assault, and as the Paras advanced, they could hear an Argentine voice calling out, possibly to give warning of this sudden attack from the west. 10 Platoon came across a lone enemy machine-gunner who lay wounded in both legs, his weapon lying abandoned beside him.

Corporal Harley of 11 Platoon caught his foot in a wire, which may have been part of a minefield, and, fearing that it might be an Argentine jumping mine, unravelled himself with some care. The platoon pushed on, skirmishing by sections until they met a concertina of wire. Fearing mines, Sappers were called for from Company Headquarters, but these could do little in the darkness except tape off the suspect area. In fact channels could be discerned between the concertinas, and these were assumed, correctly, as it turned out, to be safe lanes.

While 11 Platoon was extricating itself from the minefield, Neame pushed 12 Platoon on and brought 10 Platoon out to the left to maintain the momentum. Suddenly an intense burst of firing brought the company to a halt. It was a critical moment. For a short time, *all* commanders had to do everything in their power to get things going again, with platoon commanders and sergeants and section commanders all urging their men on. It was a real test of leadership as several soldiers understandably went to ground.

A brief fire-fight ensued, with 12 Platoon engaging the enemy as they pushed forward on the right overlooking Moody Brook below, where lights could be seen. The moment of doubt had passed, however, and once more the men were clearing bunkers and mopping up with gusto. 10 and 12 Platoons now moved on either side of the company commander. Maximum speed was needed to keep the enemy off balance as they fell back, conducting a fighting withdrawal along the ridge. The tanks continued to fire, directed by the company commander. Unfortunately his signaller had fallen into a shell hole and become separated, thus creating considerable frustration for the CO, who wanted to talk to Neame about the progress of his battle.

During 12 Platoon's brief fight Private Slough had been hit and died later in hospital, and another soldier was wounded.

Enemy artillery fire continued to make life uncomfortable. Fortunately D Company's task was no longer difficult, as most of the enemy bunkers had now been abandoned. 12 Platoon reached the telegraph wires and consolidated there, while the other platoons reorganized further back along the ridge. Shell fire intensified and snipers began to engage from enemy positions further to the east along the ridge.

Neame went up to see the platoon commander, Lieutenant Page. Snipers in the rocks were still firing on the platoon and it seemed that the enemy might be about to counter-attack from the direction of Moody Brook, to the right.

On several occasions the company commander was nearly hit, and his perambulations began to be the cause of some comment. Sergeant Meredith shouted to him, "For God's sake push off, Sir — you're attracting bullets everywhere you go!"

100 metres or so to the east, Argentines could be heard shouting to each other, as though rallying for a counter-attack. John Page called for fire support, and then ordered his own men to stop firing, for by so doing they were merely identifying their positions. They felt very isolated and vulnerable.

For two very long and uncomfortable hours the company remained under pressure. Small-arms fire mingled with all types of HE fell in and around 12 Platoon's position as the men crouched in the abandoned enemy sangars and in shell holes. John Page continued to move around his platoon, organizing its defences, and suffering a near-miss in the process. He was hit by a bullet, which passed between two grenades hanging on his webbing and landed in a full magazine in his pouch. He was blown off his feet by the shock. "It was like being hit by a sledgehammer and having an electric shock at the same time," he later described the moment. As he lay there a round exploded in the magazine, but fortunately the grenades remained intact, and he was soon on his feet.

Meanwhile the CO was still trying to get in touch with Neame to know the form. Lieutenant Webster, OC 10 Platoon, was momentarily elevated to commanding the company since he was the only officer left near Company Headquarters. As he talked to the CO, voices could be heard below in the direction of Moody Brook. Corporal

Elliot's section opened up and automatic fire was returned by perhaps ten to fifteen men. 11 Platoon moved forward to join 10 Platoon in a long extended line along the ridge, the men firing downhill towards the enemy position. Eventually the CO got through to the company commander, who had had a hair-raising time walking along the ridge to discover what was happening. He now informed the CO of his fears of imminent attack.

Sporadic enemy fire from Tumbledown added to D Company's danger, and all the earlier fears of the consequences of delay to the 5 Brigade attack came to the fore. The CO offered to send tanks up but Neame declined, since they would be very exposed on the forward slope fire positions they would be forced to adopt. He would have preferred another company to hold the first part of Wireless Ridge, which as yet remained undefended.

The company reorganized, leaving Corporal Owen's section forward as a standing patrol while 10 and 11 Platoons found dug-outs on the reverse slope. 12 Platoon stayed in its positions near the telegraph poles.

There was little more that the Companies on the northern spur could now do to support D Company. Two of A Company's trained medical orderlies had been wounded by the shelling that still continued, so the platoons had to look after their own casualties – once again the value of the medical training for all ranks was vindicated. Fortunately the helicopters in support that night were fully effective, evacuating casualties with minimum delay, and other casualties were taken back to the RAP on one of the tanks. The enemy artillery fire gave the remainder every incentive to dig, and the possibility of being overlooked by Mount Tumbledown in the morning was an additional spur.

For A and B Companies it was now a matter of lasting the cold night out, which was not without incident. Privates "Jud" Brookes and Gormley of A Company's 1 Platoon had been hit by shrapnel. The rule was to switch on the injured

The first Phantom of No 29 Squadron touches down on the runway at RAF Stanley

man's easco light, normally used for night parachute descents, to ensure that he would not be missed in the dark. Sergeant Barrett went back to look for Brookes, whose light was smashed.

"All right, Brookes – me and the Boss will be back to pick you up later."

"Ee, Sarge," he replied in a thick Northern accent, "Ah knows tha f – will."

Unknown to them, the men of 3 Platoon were actually sitting next door to thirteen Argentine soldiers, who were taking cover from their own shell-fire. Only later in the morning were they found and taken prisoner.

In B Company, the state of Privates Carroll and Philpott of 5 Platoon was a cause for concern, since both were now suffering from hypothermia after being immersed in one of the ponds. Their section commander, Corporal Steve Curtis, decided to tell the platoon commander. As he ran out into the shelling, a round exploded close by, shredding his clothes almost completely yet, amazingly, leaving him unharmed.

The mortar teams had been busy all night. By now they had moved on to the side of the A and B Company hill to avoid shelling, which had been uncomfortably close at their first position in the bottom of the valley to the north. Improvised bins had helped to reduce the tendency of the mortar tubes to bed into the soft peat, although not completely, and another problem was that tubes would at times actually slip out of their base-plates under recoil. To prevent this, mortarmen took turns to stand on the base-plates as the tubes were fired, and by the end of the night four men had suffered broken ankles for their efforts. The fire they had been able to provide was very effective, however, and all concerned had been determined that, this time, there would be no question of running short of ammunition or of being out of range. The 3 Para mortars on Longdon did sterling work providing illumination.

The Machine-Gun Platoons, too, had been hard at work, their six guns providing intense heavy fire throughout the night. Resupplied by the tanks and by the splendid work of WO2 Grace's Pioneer Platoon, they had had no worries about ammunition. But gradually the guns broke down, and by dawn only two of the six were still in action.

In Battalion Headquarters the second-in-command, the Operations Officer and Captain David Constance had taken turns at duty officer. At one point the second-in-command, Major Keeble, had been able to see the flashes of the enemy 155-mm guns as they fired, but no amount of reporting back produced any countermeasures. Once the drone of a low-flying Argentine Canberra jet was heard, and amidst the din of artillery even larger thuds reverberated as the aircraft dropped its bombs. Private Steele of the Defence Platoon was unlucky: as he lay on the ground a piece of shrapnel caught him in the back. He hardly felt it, thinking that it was only a piece of turf from the explosion – only later did he discover a rather nasty wound where the metal had penetrated.

The CO's party had not escaped either. A stray round hit Private McLoughlin, a member of the Battery Commander's group, and actually penetrated his helmet at the front. The helmet deflected the round, however, and McLoughlin walked away unharmed.

The snipers were in great demand. Their night-sights enabled them to identify the enemy infra-red sights and to use the signature that then appeared in the image itensifier as an aiming-mark. The Commando Sappers had had a relatively minor role to play in the battle, since there were no mines that it was imperative to clear. But, as at Goose Green, they provided a very useful addition when acting as infantry.

On Wireless Ridge at first light, 12 Platoon was still being sniped at from behind and to the right. Further back along the ridge, Corporal Owen had searched a command post. While rummaging in the bunker, he found a map showing all the details of the Argentine positions, as well as some patrol reports. These were quickly dispatched to Company Headquarters and on to Brigade.

Private Ferguson, in Owen's section, suddenly noticed four or five men below them. The corporal was uncertain as to who they could be — possibly 12 Platoon — and told Ferguson to challenge. The latter yelled "Who's there!", and was instantly greeted with a burst of fire that left them in no doubt. Grenades started to explode around Owen and his men as the enemy counter-attacked. The section opened fire, and Corporal Owen shouted for the machine-guns to engage.

10 Platoon meanwhile were firing on either side of the section, and Owen himself blasted away with eight M-79 rounds. The section was soon short of ammunition, and the men began to ferret for abandoned Argentine supplies. Just then the remainder of the platoon moved up to join the section; though uncertain as to exactly where the enemy were, they were determined to prevent the Argentines from regaining the ridge.

Private Lambert heard an Argentine, close in, shouting, "Grenado, grenado!"

"What a good idea," he thought, and lobbed one of his own in the direction of the voice. There were no more shouts.

11 Platoon also saw a group of four men to its front. 2nd Lieutenant Chris Waddington was unable to make out who they were and, thinking they might be 10 Platoon, shouted to them to stop. The four men took no notice, so he ordered a flare to be put up — the figures ran off as the platoon engaged with small arms and grenades. The orders not to exploit beyond the ridge-line meant that not all the enemy positions had been cleared during the night, and it seemed that some stay-behind snipers had been left there, and it was probably these that had given 12 Platoon so much trouble.

But the counter-attack, such as it was, had fizzled out. Artillery fire was called down on Moody Brook to break up any further efforts at dislodging D Company. Down below the ridge a Land Rover could be seen trying to get away. Lance-Corporal Walker fired at it and it crashed.

11 Platoon now came under extremely accurate enemy artillery fire, possibly registered on the flashes of their weapons. Major Neame therefore ordered them to cease firing with small arms, intending to continue the battle with artillery alone. Moody Brook was deserted, however. In the distance the men of D Company noticed two Argentine soldiers walking off down the track as if at the end of an exercise.

In the light of dawn it appeared to the Paras on the ridge that a large number of enemy troops were moving up to reinforce Sapper Hill to the south-east. Neame called for artillery with great urgency, but no guns were available. After a further twenty minutes or so, by which time the enemy had reached the top, the target was engaged. Meanwhile other Argentines could be seen streaming off Tumbledown and Harriet – 5 Brigade had won its battles.

As D Company began to engage this new target the CO arrived. He confirmed Neame's orders to fire on the enemy retiring towards Stanley, and the company now joined in with machine-guns in a "turkey shoot". John Greenhalgh's helicopters swept in and fired SS-11 rockets and, together with two other Scouts, attacked an Argentine battery. The enemy AA was still active, however, and all the helicopters withdrew.

The retiring Argentines on Tumbledown had made no reply to the helicopters, and their artillery had stopped. It was obvious that a major change had occurred. The news was relayed to the Brigadier, who found it difficult to believe what was happening. But the CO realised how vital it was to get the battalion moving into Stanley before the enemy could rally, and A and B Companies, together with the Blues and Royals, were ordered to move as fast as possible up on to Wireless Ridge. The Brigadier arrived, still disbelieving until Colonel Chaundler said, "It's OK, Brigadier, it's all over." Together they conferred as to what to do next. D Company ceased firing on the fleeing enemy on the far hillside, and the order was given that men were only to fire if fired upon first. Permission was then given for the battalion to move on.

B Company, by now on the ridge, was ordered down into Moody Brook. Corporal Connors's section of 5 Platoon led the way, still expecting to come under fire from the "Triple As" on the race-course. The other two sections covered him forward. He cleared the flattened buildings of the old barracks and Curtis's section took over, clearing the bridge over the Murrell River and the building on the other side, while all the time their platoon commander was exhorted, "Push on, push on!" They remained cautious, fearing booby traps or a sudden burst of fire.

A Company now took the lead as B Company, covering A's advance, moved south on to the high ground on the far side of the valley, above the road, passing through three abandoned gun positions on the way. The tanks of the Blues and Royals moved east along Wireless Ridge to give support if it should be necessary. A Company was well on the way down the road into Stanley, with C and D Companies following, when Brigade announced a cease-fire. Cheers went up, and red berets quickly replaced steel helmets. Bottles of alcohol miraculously appeared to celebrate with. Relief, elation, disbelief – all in turn had their effect.

Major Dair Farrar-Hockley led his men towards the race-course, past the abandoned guns that had been spotted so many hours earlier yet had remained operational in spite of requests for artillery fire. According to civilians afterwards, the Argentines still on the outskirts of Stanley simply broke and ran when they heard that "the Paras" were coming. The leading elements of the battalion arrived in Stanley at 1330 hours on Monday 14 June some five hours before the official cease-fire, with 2nd Lieutenant Mark Coe's 2 Platoon the first into the town. They were the first British troops into the capital.

Eventually all the companies were brought into the western outskirts, finding shelter amongst the deserted houses, a few of which had suffered from stray shells. One or two dead Argentine soldiers still lay in the street where they had been caught by shell-fire. On the race-course the Argentine flag was pulled down and Sergeant-Major Fenwick's Union Jack once more served its purpose.

Chapter Three

OPERATION THUNDERBALL

Yeshayu Ben-Porat, Eitan Haber and Zeev Schiff

J ust after midday on 27 June 1976 Air France Flight 139 was
hijacked en route to Paris from Tel Aviv by members of the
German Baader-Meinhof gang and the Popular Front for
Liberation of Palestine (PFLP). Fifteen hours later, the jet —
which had 258, mostly Israeli, passengers and crew aboard —
landed at Entebbe, in Uganda. There the four hijackers were
joined by other Baader-Meinhof and PFLP members, and
personally welcomed by President Idi Amin Dada. On the
following day, the hijackers, led by Wilfred Böse of Baader-
Meinhof, announced their demands to the waiting world: fifty-
three of their comrades, held in prisons in Israel, France, West
Germany, Switzerland and Kenya, must be released. Or they
would start shooting the hostages.

At first, the Israeli government of Yitzhak Rabin was inclined
to negotiate, since non-Jewish hostages were also involved. The
Israeli attitude changed, however, when the hijackers released all
the hostages who were not Israeli or Jewish, and it became clear
that Idi Amin Dada was intransigent in his support for the
hijackers. On 3 July, the Israeli cabinet accepted a dramatic rescue
plan proposed by Major-General Dan Shomron, general officer
commanding paratroopers and infantry.

Shomron's plan called for crack Israeli para teams to land on
the runway at Entebbe in Hercules transport planes, from which
the paratroopers, led by Lieutenant-Colonel Jonathan "Yoni"
Netanyu, would fan out to secure their targets, most importantly

the old terminal where the hostages were held. Crucial to the success of Operation Thunderball, as Shomron's plan was now called, was speed and surprise. As a ruse to fool the Ugandan airport guards, the para team detailed to take the old terminal was to drive there from the runway in a black Mercedes disguised as Amin's personal car. Meanwhile, above the airfield an Israeli Boeing would act as a mobile communications centre.

The account here of Operation Thunderball is extracted from Entebbe Rescue *by Israeli authors Ben-Porat, Haber and Schiff, and begins with the first Israeli Hercules transports landing on the runway at Entebbe, 23.01 hours, 3 July 1976.*

The lead Hercules was still taxiing slowly along the runway as a dozen soldiers leaped out and dispersed, several yards apart, on either side. Each of them turned to a nearby runway beacon and placed mobile flashlights alongside them – a precaution in case the control tower shut off the power before the other three planes landed. More soldiers charged out of the belly of the plane as it stopped moving, taking positions around it to combat any possible Ugandan reaction.

Colonel Natan Aloni was standing by the ramp of the first Hercules as it dropped open to allow in a flow of cool night air. At a distance, he could see the control tower – code-named "Aviva". With the stream of air came an army of tiny tropical flies and mosquitoes which beat against the faces of waiting infantrymen. The temperature was 60°.

Aloni, a veteran soldier, had correctly estimated that the hard work would be over as soon as the plane had landed safely. They had already come several hundred yards down the runway, and no one had opened fire. From here on, he was confident that Operation Thunderball could proceed exactly as planned. Shouting "Forward", he ran in the direction of "July" – New Terminal. The force under his command had to seize the control tower to ensure a clear takeoff at the end of the raid.

The pilot of one of the Israeli Airforce C-135 planes is carried shoulder high by well-wishers on his return with the hostages, 7th April 1976. The Israeli military censor blacked out the pilot's face and also his rank.

The mobile beacons placed by paratroops from the first plane were already illuminating the area next to runway "Yuval".

It was cramped and uncomfortable inside the Mercedes. As the pilot swung the nose of the plane around, Tzur Ben-Ami pressed down on his accelerator and the car leaped forward. Old Terminal was over to the right bathed in a pool of light. The nine men in the Mercedes knew its location, approximately 1,500 yards away, from rehearsals the day before.

Yoni shouted to the other drivers to keep in line, then ordered Tzur to drive slow enough not to arouse suspicion. Ten or fifteen seconds had already elapsed since they had left the plane, and the Mercedes was approaching the old control tower when Yoni and Tzur spotted two figures a couple of hundred yards from them.

"Pay attention now," Yoni ordered as his men gripped their weapons. The Mercedes moved straight ahead, the two Land Rovers close behind. Rain was spattering the windshield.

The two Ugandan guards were now only fifteen yards from them. During rehearsals, Yossi had insisted that Ugandan troops would not stop a Mercedes, and would certainly never fire on it; after all, these were the cars their officers used. Now, therefore, he was no less surprised than his comrades when one of the Ugandans signalled the car to halt. They were only four yards away.

The Mercedes crawled one yard nearer. This soldier could endanger the entire mission, but there was no mistaking his uplifted right arm.

A pistol poked out the right-hand window. The Ugandan fell, but wasn't dead. Nobody had heard the shot that hit him.

"Right, step on it," ordered Yoni.

Tzur Ben-Ami responded immediately.

Michael Golan steered straight into the pool of light that was Entebbe. He glided in to land and taxied straight to his preset offloading point, behind a twenty- or thirty-foot-high hillock next to one of the runways. Flicking on his microphone, Michael confirmed: "I am at 'Katie'."

Four flight controllers were on duty in the tower. Five minutes earlier, a passenger plane had asked permission to land. Now, something strange was happening to the radar screens — so foreign journalists were told later. The dancing white spots known as "snow" obscured their entire radius of sweep. Having little choice, the controllers sat back to wait patiently till the electronic disturbance abated.

"There's another light plane in the air," one of the controllers remarked, his voice clearly heard over the radios in the Hercules' cockpits. The men were instantly panicked.

Brigadier Dan Shomron had another worry. When the first Hercules braked at its assigned spot, Shomron jumped off the ramp to choose a location for his command team. The sudden silence of the Ugandan airport hit him hard. For one terrible moment, he was sure that the hostages must have been moved from Old Terminal — a fear reinforced by the memory of a crack United States army detachment that reached an American prisoner of war camp in Vietnam only to find it empty. The silence persisted as the second Hercules trundled along the runway to its parking spot.

In the defense minister's office far off in Tel Aviv, the silence seemed almost painful. The ministers sat along the walls and around the desk, some smoking, others leaning toward the intercom as if their attentiveness might coerce it into speech. But the intercom wouldn't cooperate.

Asher Ben-Natan's bottle of Napoleon brandy still stood on the desk. No one touched it. Military secretaries Braun and Poran sat with poised pens, ready to record any word coming from the intercom.

Somebody coughed, and Yitzhak Rabin turned toward him, instantly indignant, in tacit reproach for disturbing the moment.

THE SOVIET ELITE: SPETNAZ

With a peacetime complement of 30,000 combat-ready personnel, the special forces – Spetnaz – of the old USSR were the largest in the world. Controlled by Soviet Military Intelligence, the highly secretive Spetnaz specialized in assassination, sabotage and reconnaissance, working in small teams of six to eight men. A favourite weapon was the AK-74 assault rifle, fitted with silencer and flash-suppressor, an update of the famous AK-47. Spetnaz teams played a key role in Soviet seizure of Kabul in December 1979, and later fighting the fundamentalist Mujahidin in the mountains of Afghanistan. Here deep-cover teams of Spetnaz, isolated in caves for many weeks, scored some of the USSR's most spectacular successes by spotting Mujahidin infiltration routes in the Panshjir Valley, which were then eliminated in strikes by lethal Mi-24 Hind helicopter gunships and Frogfoot fighter-bombers.

Shimon Peres closed his eyes and his companions got the impression that he was offering up a silent prayer. He knew that the next ten or twenty seconds were the most critical of all – for the hostages, for the soldiers on the ground in Entebbe, for the army, and for the government of Israel.

Not far from Peres, Mota Gur was listening over his intercom to the command net on the ground in Entebbe. He could hear the first reports coming in to Dan Shomron, but was waiting for a clear picture from his head of Staff Branch, Yekutiel Adam. In the past there had been occasions when Mota had been grateful for his deputy's characteristic lack of loquaciousness, but right now he was dying to know what was happening in Entebbe.

The Israeli air force Boeing had just landed at Nairobi. The plane appeared to be an El Al jet on a scheduled flight from Johannesburg to Tel Aviv, via Nairobi. Inside the craft, doctors were installing the last items of equipment, ready for what was to come.

Kenyan security men moved in to surround the plane.

The third Hercules was a few feet above the runway when the lights went out. Pilot Ariel Luz was shocked, but only for a fraction of a second. He made a hard landing and let his plane roll forward, hoping to spot the beacons placed by the paratroops from the first plane. Then he applied his brakes, but the heavy craft only rolled to a stop on the grass beside the asphalt runway.

Michael Golan was puzzled. Only a moment ago, the runway lights had been on; now it was pitch dark. He was worried that Ugandan soldiers could creep out from the terminal buildings to attack the three planes already on the ground.

Kuti Adam, circling above in another plane, was desperate for news. He could hear Dan Shomron, could listen to reports from the teams spreading out over the airport, could grasp that the aircraft were landing without difficulties so far — but he knew nothing about the most critical stage of all. Operation Thunderball would stand or fail by what happened to the Mercedes and its companion Land Rovers. If the terrorists or Ugandans realized there were Israelis in the cars, Old Terminal could become a charnel house. Yoni Netaniahu and his men had seconds in which to reach all three entrances to the building — and Kuti Adam still had no word of them.

The fourth Hercules came in to land between the paratroop torches. In the third plane, the pilot was in a cold sweat. Beyond his windows, he saw that his front wheels had stopped three feet from a six-foot-deep trench. Three feet more and Operation Thunderball would have been over for him, his crew, and his passengers.

The Mercedes and its two Land Rover escorts were now speeding into the area between the old control tower and the terminal, close enough to see the covered walkways at the entrances, exactly as described in their preliminary briefing.

Three or four seconds ago, the second Ugandan – the one who hadn't been shot – had vanished from sight. Now he surfaced again, close to the control tower. He hadn't panicked, and he opened fire immediately. A paratroop sergeant in one of the Land Rovers loosed a burst from a Kalashnikov and the Ugandan fell.

"Faster," Yoni shouted.

Tzur Ben-Ami pressed the pedal down as far as it would go. Then the Mercedes jerked to a stop, its four doors already swinging back hard on their hinges, as the occupants shot out from the car. The spot could not have been better chosen – near enough to Old Terminal for a fast entry, but just far enough not to alert the terrorists unnecessarily.

Yoni, Yossi, and their team raced like men possessed toward the three entrances to Old Terminal.

"Those soldiers must be organizing a revolution against Amin," Jaaber commented on hearing two or three shots in the distance outside the building. This was the burst that had cut down the second Ugandan sentry.

Michel Bacos was washing his hands.

Yitzhak David straightened up on his mattress.

Lisette Hadad pulled her blanket over her head and rolled off the mattress onto the floor. Yosef Hadad grabbed a nearby chair and lifted it over his head.

Jean Jacques Maimoni, who was sitting at the far end, lifted his mattress over his body.

Yossi was the first to reach the doorway. The distance from the Mercedes took him at most three seconds. Yoni ran alongside, with the others close on his heels. Behind the rail that ran the length of Old Terminal, Yossi spotted a terrorist who had come out of the building. He fired. The terrorist bent over and ran back in the direction of the doorway.

Wilfried Böse heard the shot and came out to see what was happening. Yossi shot again, but missed. Böse leaped backward and pointed his carbine in the direction of the hostages.

"Retreat!" shouted Böse, turning his head. Yossi shot him.

"Get in," yelled Yoni. "Through the doors!"

Jaaber stood at the far end, gesturing at the terrorist girl in an unmistakable question: "What's going on?"

The girl threw her hand grenade on Jean Jacques' mattress.

Sara Davidson threw herself flat on the floor, then crawled with Uzzi and her two sons toward the corridor to the washrooms. It wasn't far, and it offered the protective sanctuary of a wall. The washrooms were already crowded with terrified hostages who had pressed themselves flat to the floor.

Hana Cohen had lost sight of her son Yaakov. In the chaos, she didn't notice that he wasn't running with her husband and daughter into the corridor. The three of them sprawled on the floor, Pasco Cohen covering his two women with his own body.

Yaakov Cohen tipped over the bench on which he had been sleeping, and covered himself with a mattress.

Ilan Hartuv ran for the corridor.

Yossi raced under the awning and up to the first door. To his horror, he found it was locked. In a fraction of a second, he spun around and hurtled toward the second entrance. He could still hear Yoni egging the others on: "Forward!

Forward!" A terrorist suddenly appeared in Yossi's way. He pressed hard on the trigger of his gun – but nothing happened. Empty magazine! Three soldiers hurtled past and into the second doorway. Yossi switched magazines in record time and jumped in after his men. Coming through the doorway, he noticed the terrorist girl standing inside the hall to the left of the door. Another instant and Yossi would have shot her, but the man behind him beat him to it. Hit by a burst, she spun onto the floor near a window. Beyond the group of hostages, who were hugging the floor, a terrorist aimed his Kalashnikov down at the spread-eagled bodies. One of the French crewmen screamed: "Don't shoot!"

The terrorist hesitated a second, and it was his last. From ten yards away, Yossi fired a burst that killed him outright.

Across to the right another terrorist managed to fire. He loosed three or four shots that echoed around the hall, then dropped. Amnon Ben-David hit him. He tried to rise and Amnon shot him again.

The paratroopers who had burst through the two open doorways could now take in a sight of utter confusion. A mad mixture of people, beds, mattresses, blankets, overnight bags. The hostages were terrified. After all, it had happened in fifteen seconds – far too quickly for anyone to grasp!

Ron Vardi and his comrades clung to the sides of a command car as it careered across the empty space to the new control tower. Off to one side was a fire station. As Ron watched, it was suddenly pitch black. Somebody had killed the airport lights. At the foot of the tower, the combat team could hear the crackle of shots from elsewhere on the field, but their target was deserted. The four flight controllers were no longer at their stations. An officer scanned the panels, searching for a switch that would restore light to the runways.

Lieutenant Shlomo Lavi raced at the head of his force, riding in two Rabbi field cars, into the Ugandan air force parking area. According to plan, his men were to prevent any attempt by the MIG pilots to get their craft airborne and attack the departing Hercules. Shlomo's mission proceeded smoothly. In minimum time the area was secure, without opposition.

Around the field, men of the Golani and the paratroop detachments were already deployed across main access routes and roads to block any reinforcements from a nearby army camp almost within earshot of Entebbe International.

At the center of the airport, Dan Shomron was losing patience. Still not a word from Yoni Netaniahu, though he could hear the crackle of light-arms fire – rarely a good sign.

Yoni's Land Rover team headed straight for the second floor. Their mission was to secure the building against any attempt to interfere with the transfer of hostages to the aircraft. The first soldier racing up met two Ugandan soldiers on the stairs. They froze. Above them, on the second floor, were more of their comrades. There was some resistance, but it was over in less than a minute and the Israelis were free to mount guard on the roof, where they could survey the entire surrounding area.

The force now inside Old Terminal had a rough idea of the number of terrorists, all of whom had to be taken care of if the evacuation was to proceed safely. While Yossi and his squad went in to the passenger hall, another team ran along the front of the building to the old VIP Room at the far end. As they arrived, the terrorists off duty came tumbling into the corridor.

Two white Europeans came out of a nearby room. For a split second Ilan Gonen held his fire, thinking that these must be passengers off the Aerobus.

"Who are you?" Ilan shouted in English.

No answer. The two men continued their slow walk.

In the defense minister's office, shots could be heard over the intercom. Were it not for the tension and anxiety, Rabin,

Peres, and the others might have found time to marvel at the wonders of modern technology that could let them listen to a battle two thousand miles away. Yet, apart from a few crisp orders issued by Dan Shomron, and terse conversations between the plane and the ground below, there was no way of knowing how things were going or whether the hostages were safe. Amos Aron was sending a message to President Ford over the phone to Ambassador Dinitz in Washington: AT THE TIME OF DELIVERY OF THIS MESSAGE, OUR FORCES . . . Dinitz listened in astonishment.

It was only at 11.07 p.m. that Kuti Adam's voice finally came through in the chief of staff's private bureau and the defense minister's room elsewhere in the building.

"Everything's okay. You'll have a precise report immediately."

Everything's okay?

What had happened at Entebbe?

Were the hostages safe?

Were the terrorists dead?

What about casualties?

The prime minister and his defense minister leaned forward, almost unable to bear the tension, praying to hear Dan Shomron's voice.

Mota Gur no longer hesitated. He called Dan directly. "What's happening there?"

"Everything's all right. I'll report later. I'm busy now."

Again, everything's all right. . . . What's all right?

Yosef Hadad held the chair over his head as protection against terrorist bullets. A bullet hit his chair, and he thought his end had come. Out of the corner of his eye, he could see Böse lying in a pool of blood.

Pasco Cohen lay on top of his wife and daughter, with more hostages on top of him. He lifted himself for a moment to make sure that Zippy wasn't suffocating. A bullet penetrated his thigh, then tore an artery near his bladder.

"I'm wounded," he told Hana quietly, "look after the children."

As Pasco collapsed on the floor of the corridor, Jean Jacques Maimoni panicked at the sight of the hand grenade that had landed on his mattress. The boy jumped to his feet and ran, bent over, toward the washroom corridor. Two bullets hit his back and sent him sprawling on the floor, dead. Yitzhak David, who lifted his body in an attempt to pull Jean Jacques down, took a bullet in his shoulder.

"Who are you?" Ilan Gonen yelled again. But the two Europeans went on walking, as though all the hubbub and chaos had nothing to do with them. The soldier pointed his gun barrel at them. Spotting the flash of a grenade fuse, he let loose a burst, then dropped flat on the floor. The grenade exploded in the corridor, tearing the bodies of the two Europeans but not harming the paratroopers.

Sara Davidson thought she could hear voices speaking Hebrew. They were coming nearer! A loudspeaker boomed through the enclosed space: "This is *Zahal* — the IDF! We've come to take you home! Lie on the floor and wait for instructions! This is *Zahal!*"

Yosef Hadad shouted in a voice clearly heard throughout Old Terminal: "They're ours! They're ours!"

Somebody else lifted a head to call: "Israeli soldiers? Israeli soldiers!"

Baruch Gross peeked into the hall from the washroom corridor and almost stopped breathing. Before him stood an Israeli soldier. There could be no mistake! But the man's gun was pointing at him. Baruch didn't lose his head: "*Yisrael!*" he shouted the Hebrew word, "*Yisrael!*" The gun barrel turned, and it seemed to Baruch that his life was also turning.

"Lie on the floor," boomed the bullhorn, "we have come to get you and it will be all right!"

Thirteen-year-old Benny Davidson couldn't believe it. Only at noon he had jokingly told his parents and brother that "the army will come to free us tonight at midnight." So he had said it — so what? He didn't mean it, and certainly didn't believe it. And now, one hour before midnight, Israeli soldiers had appeared in Old Terminal. Sara Davidson dropped on top of Ron, while Benny mumbled a prayer.

Hana Cohen didn't lose her head. She was too good a nurse for that. Tearing Pasco's shirt, she bandaged the wound, but the makeshift dressing turned red. The wound was deep. Pasco was losing too much blood.

Yossi ran through Old Terminal checking to see that all the terrorists were dead. Then he called a sixteen-year-old hostage named Michael, and asked him to identify them. Once that was done, Yossi reported to Brigadier Dan Shomron, somewhere on Entebbe's field. Shomron passed the news on to Yekutiel Adam in the Boeing. Adam relayed the message to General Gur. "The transgressors are eliminated," he said quietly. "I repeat, transgressors eliminated."

Four words were all it took to relieve the tension in Shimon Peres' study. A smile flittered across Yitzhak Rabin's face, and Shimon Peres' eyes sparkled. But they still didn't know very much.

The men in the room could now allow themselves a few words of quiet conversation, but their voices were muted. Suddenly the phone rang; General Zeevi from Paris. He was still waiting for new instructions. Who the hell could negotiate this way? Could he please speak to the prime minister?

This time Rabin told Gandhi that there was no more need for French mediation, and he hoped that the general would forgive him for not saying anything sooner. As a military man of many years' standing, Gandhi could understand Rabin's earlier predicament. And he would be delighted to accept the honor of personally informing President Giscard d'Estaing.

On the second floor of Old Terminal, paratroops checked room by room, looking for terrorists or Ugandan troops.

Their instructions were to allow the Ugandans to escape, provided of course they didn't offer resistance. Scores of black troops made use of the opportunity to get away, and quickly.

Almost all the Israeli vehicles were now headed toward the old control tower. First place was given to the half-track armored personnel carrier, from which a torrent of lead from bazooka rockets and machine-gun bullets poured onto the tower. Its occupants had been firing on the Israelis for the past few minutes, and the paratroopers could not but admire the courage of the unknown defenders. Finally it seemed that stage two could begin: the hostages could be moved out to the plane that would take them home.

Only now did Yossi realize that he hadn't heard Yoni's voice for at least sixty seconds. He scanned the interior of Old Terminal, but there was no sign of his commanding

---

SAS: MEDITERRANEAN RAIDERS

Formed in 1941 as an irregular hit-and-run force, the British Special Boat Squadron (SBS) had an almost unrivalled elan. This was perfectly captured in an incident where a junior SBS officer, Andy Clark, landed on a German-occupied island in the Greek Aegean and walked to the Wehrmacht officers mess, opened the door and said to the astonished assembly, 'It would all be so much *easier* if you would just raise your hands'. Clark almost pulled the stunt off, but one quick-witted German grabbed a Luger pistol and started shooting. Luckily, Clark had brought his Glaswegian sergeant with him, who promptly subdued the room with submachine gun fire.

---

officer. Running from the building, he found Yoni almost immediately. He lay unconscious on the ground by the building, a doctor and a corpsman in attendance, trying to save his life. He had been shot in the very first minutes after leaving the Mercedes – a bullet in the back, fired from the old control tower, the place that had worried him during yesterday's rehearsal. Yoni had dropped to the ground, mortally wounded, a moment after guiding his men to target.

Yossi, startled to realize that he was now in command of the main force in Operation Thunderball, begged the doctor: "Do everything you can!"

Inside the lead Hercules, Dr. Yosef was getting anxious. He knew that the aircraft now made a huge static target as it sat being filled with fuel. It was vulnerable even without the flashes of firing that the doctor could see through the small portholes. With him were nine more doctors and orderlies, waiting up front for the hostages, praying they weren't wounded – but ready to do their jobs if they had to.

Yitzhak David rubbed his shoulder. Blood was pouring from it. Ilan Hartuv suddenly noticed the sticky red stream, and raised his voice over the din: "Our leader is hurt. Someone come and bandage him." Michael helped Ilan bind the wound and brought him over to the mattress where, until yesterday, his mother had slept. It was empty, but next to it lay Ida Borowitz, her son Boris stooping over her.

Ida's body was covered with blood. Nobody had noticed her die, but the body of a terrorist lay beside her. Had he shot her? Had he decided to die with one of the hostages? Boris hugged the dead body of his mother and wailed: "*Imaleh, Imaleh* – Mother, Mother!" There were tears in the eyes of the people around him, yet the time had not yet come to mourn the dead.

Sergeant Hershko Surin was due to begin demobilization leave the next day, Sunday. His three years of conscript service were almost over. Twelve hours before ending his military career, Hershko dashed into Entebbe Old Terminal.

Climbing the stairs to the second floor, he met two Ugandans. One of them was faster than Hershko. Sergeant Surin dropped to the ground, wavering between life and death, his body paralyzed.

By the outer wall of Old Terminal, a doctor labored to save Yoni Netaniahu. It was useless. The brilliant young lieutenant colonel who had come home to serve his people was dying. Yossi Yaar and the others lifted him gently onto a stretcher. For a moment it seemed that Yoni's will to live might overcome. He raised his head as though wanting to say something — then dropped back on the stretcher.

Yossi ordered his men to collect the casualties strewn across the floor. The bodies of Ida Borowitz and Jean Jacques Maimoni were laid on stretchers, as were the ten people injured in the course of the lightning-fast raid. Bullhorns summoned all the hostages back from corridors and side rooms into the main hall. The stunned men, women, and children shuffled in. The paratroopers had to slap a few to bring them out of shock.

The pilot of the first Hercules started his engines and began to move his craft slowly and cautiously toward Old Terminal, stopping 500 yards away. Yossi ordered his men to prepare the evacuation of the wounded and the hostages, although shots were still being exchanged between Israeli soldiers and Ugandans. When it seemed that the gunfire had finally stopped, Yossi picked up a bullhorn and instructed the hostages to check and see that all members of their families were accounted for.

Uzzi Davidson collected together Sara, Benny, and Ron. Yitzhak David, lying on a stretcher, grasped his wife's hand.

Ilan Hartuv was very worried. His mother was still in Mulago Hospital, but what could be done about that?

Outside the terminal, soldiers took position in two lines, forming a funnel straight to the gaping hatch of the Hercules. Yoni's solution for shock and panic would still be used, even if he wasn't there to supervise it. Yet there was another reason: no one wanted a hostage to run into an engine.

Command cars, jeeps, Rabbi field cars, and a Peugeot pickup truck pulled into the area in front of the building as the 104 hostages were started moving toward the waiting plane. There was some panic. Families clung together and rushed for the vehicles. One young girl came out dressed only in bra and panties, as there had been no time to dress. A soldier threw her a blanket, and she wrapped it around herself as she scrambled onto a command car. Shots were still being fired.

Eighteen minutes had passed since the Mercedes began its journey across Entebbe Airport. Now Yekutiel Adam's voice boomed out from a radio in the General Staff "pit", and from the intercoms in Gur's and Peres' rooms: "Mount Carmel. I repeat, Mount Carmel!"

The prime minister and defense minister knew now that the tough part of the mission was almost over. "Mount Carmel" was the code word denoting the start of evacuation from Old Terminal.

Defense Ministry spokesman Naftali Lavi dialled the home of a military correspondent of one of the daily papers. "It's worthwhile to stay awake tonight," he said — but refused to elaborate.

"What's happening?"

Naftali could not explain, so he merely said, "They'll trade terrorists for hostages tonight."

The journalist couldn't swear to it, but there seemed to be a note of mockery in the spokesman's last remark.

The 500 yards now appeared secure, so Yossi gave the signal for the vehicles to move. Across the way, the engines of the Hercules were holding to a steady, muffled roar. Hostages who hadn't found places on the vehicles began to walk toward the plane.

Hana Cohen swept Zippy up in her arms and began to run. Yaakov caught up with her and ran alongside. Pasco, lying on a stretcher, waved weakly to his son as he was lifted inside the Hercules. A team of doctors and orderlies set to work at once to save his life, pushing Hana, who wanted to help, gently aside. Before she even found a seat, she could see a blood-transfusion bag in place as the precious fluid dripped into Pasco's body. The wound was evidently more serious than she had realized.

Dr Yosef leaned over the stretcher that bore the unconscious body of Lieutenant Colonel Jonathan Netania-hu. There was nothing more that could be done. Yoni was dying, and the doctors were powerless to prevent it happening.

Soldiers helped hostages off the vehicles by the ramp of the Hercules, guiding them across the 500-yard walk. Their stunned charges were encouraged to move at a brisk pace, yet there was no need for panic.

Inside the cockpit, the pilot and his crew were already making their pre-takeoff instrument check. Behind them, at the bottom of the ramp, officers and men of the Thunderball force quietly asked each hostage to check that all his family were accounted for. When Captain Bacos approached the ramp, an officer politely asked him to check his family — the crew of Air Force 139. No one was missing. Only Ilan Hartuv remained silent. He was leaving his mother behind in a Ugandan hospital, with no way to save her — but what else could he do? It would be futile to remain in Entebbe. Now, in the doorway of the Hercules, he could only hope that the president of Uganda would extend his protection to Dora Bloch. Still stunned by the events of the last half hour, Ilan pressed forward into the belly of the plane. Like the others, he was still finding it difficult to believe that the week of captivity was nearly over.

Far away across the airport, Lieutenant Shlomo Lavi and his men detailed to guard the Ugandan MIGs were firing at

Ugandan soldiers coming from the direction of the terminal. The opposition was heavy enough to force Lavi's team into equally heavy return fire.

Michael Golan, in the cockpit of the second Hercules, was still behind the hillock next to a runway. The MIGs were parked in a lower area of the airport and he couldn't see them, although he did notice flames and a column of smoke ascending into the night sky. It was Shlomo Lavi's men blowing up eleven MIGs – seven 21s and four 17s. Perhaps half the order of battle of the Ugandan air force was now smoke and ashes.

A spirited radio conversation began between Michael and the other three pilots. Minutes ago an attempt had started to refuel the Israeli planes from Entebbe Airport storage tanks. They had brought three pumps and a group of men who had served in Uganda and knew exactly where the airport fuel stocks were kept. One of the planes was already linked up, but the pump was supplying fuel at low pressure. It seemed as if the process was going to take forty-five minutes, and the pilots were growing nervous. Finally, the Golani detachment commander radioed a suggestion to Dan Shomron to stop the refuelling: "We have succeeded. Why should we take more risks here?"

Kuti and Benny heard the conversation and agreed, ordering immediate takeoff. Never mind reloading the pumps! All of them together are only worth ten thousand dollars! Let Amin have them. Get those planes airborne!

The lead Hercules, with its load of dazed hostages, lumbered onto the long runway, gathered speed, and climbed heavily into the night. In the cockpit, the hands of the clock indicated 11.43; precisely forty minutes after the first plane landed at Entebbe.

"'Hear, O Israel . . .'" One of the passengers recited the ancient prayer, and Baruch Gross picked up the refrain.

Chapter Four

THE STAND
AT IMJIN RIVER

A. H. Farrar-Hockley and E. L. Capel

T *he Stalinist regime of North Korea launched a major offensive in the Korean War on 22 April 1951, breaking through the line held by the United Nations west of Chungpyong Reservoir. The situation was only saved by the stand of the Gloucestershire Regiment at Imjin River against a much larger enemy force, composed mostly of Chinese communists. The Glosters' action was later termed "the most outstanding example of unit bravery in modern warfare" by the UN Commander in Korea, General James Van Fleet. A. H. Farrar-Hockley, the co-author of this account of the Glosters' stand was the Adjutant of the regiment during the Imjin River battle.*

The battalion moved back towards the battle line on 21 March 1951, a monumental date for the past and, did they but know it, for the future. But the first step towards the Imjin river was neither very demanding nor challenging: Colonel Carne was ordered to site and dig a battalion position covering Uijongbu. The sector belonged to the 3rd United States Division and its Commander was anxious to have a long stop on the road leading south from the river through the hills at this point. Though little more than a rough track it had been used successfully by the Chinese less than three months previously as a main thrust line to Seoul. It was, indeed, an ancient invasion route by the armies of Imperial China. So the Glosters dug and wired, grumbling cheerfully as British soldiers do when they are obliged to prepare defences without an enemy in sight.

Even when, at the beginning of April, they moved north through the hills along this route to the Imijin itself, there was no sign of the enemy, and this was in many ways a comfort; for though the river formed the front edge of the UN defensive line "Kansas", there were so few troops to man it that the gap between the Glosters' left and the nearest ROK unit was three miles. On the right, the nearest friendly element was a company of the Fifth Fusiliers, almost two miles distant. Thus isolated, the battalion was required to deny to the Communist Forces, the use of the road running south.

The Glosters relieved the PEFTOK (Phillipines Expeditionary Force, Task Organisation Korea) and these small brown, friendly, men withdrew to the south. They had been in the position only a few days and had very little intelligence about enemy locations or strengths. It seemed to Colonel Carne that he had better do something to remedy this lack of knowledge as soon as his companions had settled. "A" Company, under Major Pat Angier, was left forward on the old Castle Site, a high point (148) west of the village of Choksong. "D" under Major "Lakri" Wood, were on the hill feature south-east of the village. "B" Company, commanded by Major Denis Harding, somewhat to the east guarded the right flank approaches. "C" (Major Paul Mitchell) lay in reserve on the high ground directly above battalion headquarters. The headquarters site was at a point where the road running south entered the hills and swung across a shallow stream. The open valley mouth towards the river was held by the Drums. Troubled by a triangular-shaped height immediately to the west overlooking this site, the colonel put out on it his only uncommitted force, the assault pioneers under Captain "Spike" Pike.

It was a carefully considered deployment which made the best of a frontage of seven miles and depth of five. Any

Men of the 1st Battalion, the Gloucestershire Regiment take up new positions

enemy approach would lie through the small arms fire of at least two companies, and two sections of the Vickers machine-guns. The guns of 45 Field Artillery Regiment, backed potentially by the United States 3rd Divisional artillery, the mortars of "C" Troop, 170 Mortar Battery and the Glosters own 3-inch mortar platoon were able between them to cover both companies and approaches with shell or bomb. The difficulty was to detect enemy movement by night. A change in darkness to a tight defensive position was not practicable because of the shortage of defence stores. It took eight days to get the first truck load of barbed wire and the second did not reach the battalion until it had been in position for seventeen days. Much had happened in that time.

An active patrol programme confirmed that the ford across the Imjin river, carrying the road from Seoul northwards, was intact and the enemy defences covering it on the far bank empty. But there had been movement in the high ground immediately to the north amongst a series of bunkers. "A" and "D" Companies combined in a night operation to close on these and sweep them at dawn. Apart from a radio mishap at the outset, this was most successful, though when the troops searched the bunkers these were also found to be abandoned. Where had the enemy gone?

A major sortie followed in daylight: two company groups and Major George Butler's squadron on the 8th Hussars moved north across the Imjin to a distance of seven miles in an operation named "Cygnet" – young swan. At last a few half-starved and very miserable Chinese soldiers were captured. Was this the rearguard of the mighty Chinese Peoples' Volunteers?

As a matter of fact it was. Weakened by the severity of the winter and defeated by the advancing United Nations forces, the mass of Chinese divisions had broken away from their pursuers during March. There had thus been no pursuit into the heart of North Korea as in 1950. General

Ridgway had now replaced General Macarthur as Supreme Commander, Allied Powers, and his orders were to hold on or about the line of the 38th Parallel of latitude – the old demarcation line between north and south – which, in this sector, was roughly along the course of the Imjin. A few exhausted Chinese and North Korean units had been left to hold an outpost line while, twenty miles to the north over a period of six weeks, the Chinese commander-in-chief, Peng Teh-Huai, refreshed, replenished, and reinforced his armies. Then, with the winter finally past, he gave orders on 13 April for a fresh offensive. Small reconnaissance parties were sent south to discover and infiltrate between the UN positions, travelling only by night, resting and watching by day. On the night of the 21st, the mass of the attacking armies began to march south after them, amongst them the 63rd Army of three divisions[1] – the 187, 188, 189 – with orders to force open the ancient route to Seoul . . .

Various sources of intelligence had disclosed to the United Nations commander in Korea, General James van Fleet, that an offensive was impending. All units were ordered to be ready and thus all were watchful. A little after midday on 22 April, the Glosters' artillery observation posts saw twenty enemy moving south in file . . . dressed in dark uniforms. Larger body of men moved round behind hill . . . immediately north of the Imjin ford known as Gloster Crossing. Air recce began to search as Colonel Carne accompanied a patrol to a vantage point close to the river from which to observe. The adjutant joined the colonel and the intelligence officer, Lieutenant Henry Cabral, on the bank. Five more enemy parties between ten and twenty strong were observed occupying the old positions on the high ground immediately to the north, in which they were

---

[1] A Chinese Communist Forces (CCF) Division was about 9,000 strong mostly infantry with six to eight batteries of light artillery and about twice this number of medium and heavy mortars.

HANOVERIAN FUSILIERS:
THE STORM OF STEEL

The prototype Special Forces were the *sturmtruppen,* or 'storm troopers', developed by the German Army on the Western Front in 1915. Intended to be an hard-hitting but extremely mobile assault force, the storm troopers carried little kit aside from the tools of their trade: stick grenade in sacks, gas mask, entrenching tool and a Kar 98 rifle (towards the end of the war, this was replaced by the Bergmann MP 18.1 submachine gun). The storm troopers were also highly trained. As one storm troop officer, Ernst Junger, recorded in his wartime diary, he demanded that his storm trooper company of the 73rd Hanoverian Fusiliers trained with absolute realism: 'Sometimes I made practice attacks with the company on complicated trench systems, with live bombs'. Casulties were frequent. In 1918 the German storm troopers led the Michael Offensive, punching a hole in the British line. However, the assault units became starved of supplies and artillery support and were unable to consolidate their impressive gains.

---

severely shelled. But otherwise the colonel's orders, sent back to the adjutant, were clear: the companies were to take pains to lie low and conceal themselves from what were obviously enemy scouting parties. A fighting patrol was to be prepared in "C" Company — one platoon — to lay an ambush on the south side of the ford as soon as it was dark. Meantime, "A" Company's observation post was to watch this sensitive point until dusk and to shell and mortar any attempt to seize it in daylight.

The afternoon passed in an atmosphere of excitement. Everyone in the battalion sensed that a major clash was imminent. Men rested in all positions. At 5 p.m. the hot evening meal was eaten and before dusk a comprehensive check of weapons and ammunition had been completed. Half the reserve ammunition was brought forward from "A" Echelon to the headquarters site. As the light waned, the ambush party from "C" Company, Lieutenant Guy Temple's platoon, came down from their hilltop and made their way to the river and ford.

The task of the "C" Company platoon was to surprise and destroy the enemy attempting to cross to the south of the Imjin. It was only partially successful for two reasons. First, because the weight of the enemy seeking to cross were far greater than had been expected from air reconnaissance and ground observation reports during the afternoon and evening. At dusk on the 22 April, the main body of the enemy were not within twelve miles of the river. They closed on the Imjin in a forced march of three hours carrying all their battle gear. Lieutenant Temple's platoon destroyed the enemy's advanced party attempting to seize the crossing by *coup de main* early in the night but were then pressed by a battalion backed by two more. 70 Field Battery, "C" Troop of 170 Mortar Battery, the mortar platoon and the small arms of the ambush fired continuously for some hours but they could not stem indefinitely the flood of Chinese soldiers.

Meantime, unknown to the Glosters, a second enemy brigade was crossing the Imjin at another ford, of which they were unaware, one-and-a-half miles down stream. This was the second reason for the limited success of the ambush and a consequence of the excessive frontage held by the battalion. Even while the ambush held the enemy to its front in check, a strong assault was being launched against "A" company on the Castle Site by about two battalions while a third crossed the road to the east to attack "D" Company.

Up stream, the left flank company of the Fifth Fusiliers holding a ridge overlooking the river and lateral road had been attacked and forced to withdraw. A battalion from this area moved south to attack "B" Company of the Glosters. Not long after midnight, therefore, the three forward rifle companies of the Glosters were in action, "A" Company being critically pressed by an enemy outnumbering them by six to one.

At battalion headquarters, Captain Reeve-Tucker, the signals officers, entered the command vehicle with a message from the ambush party.

"They're still trying to cross in hordes, sir," he said to the colonel. "In another five minutes, he [Temple] reckons they'll be out of ammunition."

The colonel looked across at Major Guy Ward, the battery comander, and the adjutant.

"Tell him to start withdrawing in three minutes," he said to the adjutant. "Guy, I'm going to ask you for one last concentration, and then start dropping them short of Gloster Crossing as soon as the patrol is back at the first cutting south of the river."

The advantage of the United Nations' Forces as their line was, almost everywhere, assailed that night was in the power of their weapons, particularly artillery, to drop destructive fire accurately into the enemy masses. Their weakness lay in the length of front which resulted in numbers of fragmented battles, each of which needed to be won by the defence if Line Kansas was to be held. The artillery could not engage so many targets adequately. The morning light would permit the UN air forces to add their weight of fire power. The question was, would it be enough?

At a number of points, air strikes forced the enemy to withraw temporarily by 9 a.m. on the morning of the 23rd but there were none available to the Glosters.

Before dawn on the 23rd the battalion Command Post had moved up to the ridge held by "C" Company. From there, in a bunker constructed under RSM Jack Hobbs' supervision some days before, the colonel could overlook the battle on the two hill positions to the north. The desperate nature of the struggle was manifest before the morning sun rose. By night, the calls for fire support, each fresh report from "A", "B" or "D" Company headquarters and the artillery radio links had made it all too clear that the attack was in strength. Just after dawn, in the command post, Corporal Walters told the adjutant that Major Angier, commanding "A" Company, wished to speak to him.

"I'm afraid we've lost the Castle Site. I'm mounting a counter-attack now but I want to know whether to expect to stay here indefinitely or not. If I am to stay on, I must be reinforced as my numbers are getting very low."

When the message was passed to the colonel he was already considering what his options were now that daylight had come. Two questions were in his mind: would the Chinese continue to press their attack in daylight with the threat of intervention by UN aircraft; and, secondly, how long would it be before the Chinese discovered that both battalion flanks were completely open and encircle his battalion?

He questioned Major Angier briefly and then gave his orders:

"You will stay there at all costs until further notice."

At all costs and until further notice . . . The need for "A" Company to hold its position was this: notwithstanding the loss of the highest point of their position, they had still observation over the approaches to "D" Company as well as forward to the two river crossing points. If the company was precipitately withdrawn, the Chinese would reinforce freely the force on the south bank, overwhelm "D" Company, and in turn, "B".

The adjutant sent forward a supply of ammunition in a pair of Oxford carriers under Lieutenant Cabral.

"Don't worry about us," said Major Angier on the radio; "we'll be all right." He returned to the fight. The counter-attack was in progress to regain the Castle Site on which, in one of the company's bunkers, the Chinese had installed a medium machine-gun. Lieutenant Philip Curtis led his platoon forward as the guns of 70 Field Battery fired in support. But the overhead cover in the bunker protected the enemy machine-gun crew and they fired freely into the attacking platoon, driving them back within half a minute. Amongst the wounded dragged into cover was Lieutenant Curtis. Corporal Papworth of the Royal Army Medical Corps began to attend to the injuries. Curtis did not wait for his attention.

"We must take the Castle Site," he said.

"Just wait until Papworth has seen you, sir," said a soldier at his side. But he would not wait. Alone he ran forward painfully, a pistol in one hand, a grenade in the other. Possibly waiting until this single figure advancing reached point blank range the Chinese machine-gunners held their fire. Curtis pulled the pin from his grenade and threw it. As it flew through the air, the Chinese opened fire and killed him; but were themselves killed a few seconds later as the grenade landed directly in the bunker opening and blew away the muzzle of their gun. Then, as Major Angier was directing a platoon to close upon this key point, he was killed and command of the company passed to the only suriving officer, Lieutenant Terry Waters. By the time he came up to take over, the opportunity to recover the Castle Site had passed.[1]

To the east, "D" Company was under command of Captain M. G. Harvey.[2] By about 8.30 on that morning, 23 April, it was apparent that neither "A" nor "D" Companies could hold against the weight of successive attacks unless air support was available. At 7.30, the brigade commander had given permission to Colonel Carne to

[1] Lieutenant Curtis was to receive a posthumous Victoria Cross for his gallantry.
[2] Major W. A. Wood was away with a leave party in Japan.

74

withdraw his forward positions. When it became clear about fifty minutes later that the Glosters' request for air strikes would not be satisfied, the colonel gave the order to withdraw. "A" and "D" Companies were brought into positions immediately north-west and west of battalion headquarters and "B" Company to a hill feature below the great height of Kamak-San to the east of the road.

In breaking away from the enemy, the whole fire potential of the battalion, Captain Frank Wisbey's heavy mortar troop and the three batteries of 45 Field Regiment was used against the enemy of the 187 CCF Division. Their dead and wounded lay in heaps on the hill slopes they had occupied and in the gulleys along which they had sought to infiltrate past the main position. With "A" and "D" Company positions in their hands, they had had enough and by noon the battlefield fell quiet.

The adjutant recalled a series of incidents of that day, "clear in themselves but joined by a very hazy thread of continuity . . ."

Color Sergeant Buxcey organizing his Korean porters with mighty loads for the first of many ascents to the new "A" company positions . . . When Buxcey's anxious face has left my mind, I can still see Captain Bob Hickey, the doctor, working at the Regimental Aid Post, one hand still wet with blood as he turns round, pausing for a moment to clean himself before he begins to minister to yet another wounded man. The ambulance cars are filled; the jeep that Bounden drives has been out time and again with the stretchers on its racks. Sergeants Baxter and Brisland, Corporal Mills, the whole staff of the RAP is hard at work with dressings, drugs, and instruments . . . I remember watching the slow, wind-tossed descent of a helicopter that came down for casualties to whom the winding, bumpy road back south would have meant certain death . . . Shaw, my

driver, and Mr Evans, the Chief Clerk, went off to Seoul .
. . Captain Carl Dain, the counter-mortar radar officer
came in to say, "I'm sending my vehicles back, except for
my jeep. I've decided to stay with you to make up your
numbers of Forward Observation Officers . . ." Lieutenant Donald Allman, the assistant adjutant, was sent to
reinforce "A" company, now under its second-in-command, Captain Anthony Wilson . . . That morning the
Padre, Sam Davies, said a funeral service for Pat Angier,
whose body had been brought back on one of the
Oxford carriers by Lieutenant Cabral. Pat's body was
the only one to which we could pay our last respects —
but we did not forget the others. Three of us stood by
while the solemn words were said: then we saluted and
walked away, each busy with his own thoughts.

Pat lay at rest beside the soft-voiced stream, quiet in
the morning sunlight.

Later that morning, the battalion second-in-command, Major
Digby Grist, came forward to see what was to be done by way
of support for the battle which must surely come to life again
as soon as darkness fell. While discussing the prospect, news
came that rear battalion headquarters ("A" Echelon) five miles
back, had been attacked and forced to withdraw: the enemy
had infiltrated strong patrols this far south. The colonel said, "I
think you'd better go back at once, Digby, to see what is
happening." Well aware that he was almost certainly about to
run a gauntlet of fire, the second-in-command set off calmly
with his driver, Bainbridge. Thirty minutes later, they were
driving for their lives through an enemy ambush.

On the right flank, Major Harding had managed to withdraw from his former position secretly and his new site was
unknown to the enemy. He was determined not to reveal it
until compelled to do so. When observers reported the
approach of enemy patrols, Sergeant Pethrick was sent out
to lay an ambush on the most likely approach. Not long after he

had settled, expecting to catch a patrol, about 200 Chinese obligingly entered his position and a fire fight began. The Chinese, part of 188 CCF Division, reinforced and began to work round the flanks of the ambush. Sgt Pethrick was ordered back while other detachments from his company went forward, greatly assisted by medium and heavy mortar fire, to hold the enemy off the main position. Backwards and forward, all among the little kolls that lay below the peak of Kamak-San, engagements flared up and died, only to be renewed elsewhere.

Notwithstanding the capture of the forward company positions of the Glosters, the commander of 63 CCF Army was disastisfied, as we are now aware, with the progress of his force after twenty-four hours of attack. The 187 Division had failed to destroy the battalion holding the old road running south through Solma-ri. On the night of 23/24 April, it had been planned that 188 Division should march down this road to cut in behind the bulk of the British 29th Brigade and the 3rd United States Division. Due to the casualties inflicted on the 187 Division, the 188 had now to complete the elimination of the Glosters though, as the battle line stood, the tactical opportunity seemed still to be open to the 63rd Army. The 29th Brigade and 3rd Division were fighting in positions east north east of the Glosters: if the latter could be disposed of during the first hours of darkness of that night, it should prove possible to march rapidly down the road to Uijongbu. For this reason, Chinese patrolling and probing attacks began early in the evening, particularly against "B" Company, with the aim of finding a route into the heart of the battalion's position and a bypass along which part of the division might slip to the south.

Under the arrangements of Sergeant Smythe, the signal sergeant, telephone cables had been run to all new company positions. At ten minutes to midnight on 23 April, Major Denis Harding telephoned the battalion command post.

"Well, we've started. They're attacking Beverly's [Lieutenant Gael's] platoon now — about 150 I should think."

This explained the noise from this direction. Captain "Recce" Newcome, the artillery FOO, was directing defensive fire from the guns. From "C" Company came similar news. The 188 Division was attempting to force the right flank of the battalion while simultaneously making for the highest ground in the area, the peak of Kamak-San. In character, the assaults on the rifle companies followed the pattern of the previous night: wave after wave of men armed with grenades and sub-machine guns stormed the positions under cover of medium machine-guns and mortar fire, were halted by the fire of the defence – small arms, mortars, guns – and driven back with heavy loss.

At the outset of the engagement on the night of 23/24 April, the Chinese were at a disadvantage. The information gained by their patrols was faulty largely due to Major Harding's deceptive tactics: they attacked late and obliquely the battalion right flank so that the assaults, pressed blindly for the first few hours, were struck by enfilade fire. Some time after two o'clock in the morning of the 24th there was a lull during which it seems probable that a fresh regiment came forward, with a truer idea of the Glosters' positions.

About a quarter to three, intense enemy mortar and machine-gun fire fell among "B" and "C" Companies. The soldiers waiting – regulars, national servicemen, recalled reservists; west countrymen predominantly, with a scattering from London and almost every other county of the British isles; but long since moulded in comradeship by the fortunes of war – stood to their weapons to face another onslaught. Despite the slaughter inflicted on the enemy by their courage and skill, the Glosters' numbers were dwindling. There seemed to be no limit to the casualties the Chinese commanders were prepared to sacrifice to their aim. There was a limit to the casualties that the British battalion could accept if it was to sustain an effective defence.

At three o'clock the telephone from "C" Company rang in the command post. Major Paul Mitchell spoke to the adjutant.

"I'm afraid they've overrun my top position and they're reinforcing hard. They're simply pouring chaps in above us. Let me know what the colonel wants me to do, will you?"

The colonel had no doubt as to what had to be done. With the enemy in strength on the commanding ground of "C" Company's ridge, the right half of the battalion had been cracked open. Below this lay the headquarters site with the radios connecting the battalion to brigade headquarters and the guns, the regimental aid post with the wounded sent down during the night, the battalion 3-inch mortars and the artillery heavy mortars.

"Pack the headquarters up," the colonel said to the adjutant, "and get everyone out of the valley up between 'D' Company and the anti-tank platoon position. I'm going to withdraw 'C' Company in ten minutes; and I shall move 'B' over to join us after first light."

The withdrawal of "C" Company was an extremely difficult operation in darkness, and as a result only one third of the Company eventually joined the battalion on Hill 235 — the final position.

By dawn, all but "B" Company were on the high ground overlooking the valley from the west. The next problem was to disengage "B" Company and bring them into the main position; a taxing problem because they were still under attack. By fortunate chance, the local Chinese commander decided to concentrate his force against one platoon, Lieutenant Geoffrey Costello's, and no less fortunately Costello's platoon held firm, the wounded standing with the unwounded. Across the valley in the main position, Captain Dain was able to bring shellfire down amongst the Chinese infantry scrambling up the hillside and Sergeant Syke's section of Vickers opened fire effectively into this target at 2,000 yards range. At first slowly and painfully, Major Harding managed to draw away what remained off his company. With the rearguard of Lieutenant Arthur Peal's platoon, Harding himself broke away at last. A group of the enemy followed them, closing as they approached the foot of the Glosters' hill but were driven back as Private "Lofty" Walker of "C" Company, entirely of his own initiative, ran down to meet them, firing a Bren light machine-gun from the hip into the approaching foe. Twenty of "B" Company survived the journey. Colonel Carne combined them with the remnant of "C" Company under Major Harding's command.

During and after the movement of "B" Company, three important matters had to be attended to: the detailed knitting together of the defences in the new position on Hill 235[1] against renewed attack; the clarification of the battalion's position in relation to the remainder of the battle in the sector; and a check of physical resources in weapons, ammunition, radio batteries, water, medical supplies and food. The colonel was engaged in the first between seven o'clock on the morning of the 24th, when the sun broke through a haze of grey clouds, and 8.45. His round of the battalion was not without incident. Prior to "B" Company's move he came across a group of Chinese infiltrating forward and, supported by two of the regimental police and his driver, he drove them back with the loss of two dead.

"What was all that about, sir?" asked his adjutant as he came back over the ridge.

"Oh, just shooing away some Chinese." He continued on his way. A few minutes later, the brigade major[2] came on to the radio to answer the adjutant's request for information about tactical intentions. He had cheering news. PEFTOK — the Filipinos — were on their way forward to reinforce the battalion and on 25 April armour and infantry in brigade strength would come up in relief. The battalion should be back in reserve by the evening of the 25th.

Meantime, it had to maintain its powers of defence. An

---

[1] Later to be called Gloster Hill.
[2] Major Jim Dunning, who was acting in place of Major K. R. S. Trevor, on leave.

expedition was arranged to descend the steep path to the headquarters site to collect ammunition and all the other supplies which were needed. RSM Jack Hobbs and CSMI "Muscles" Strong of the Army Physical Training Corps assembled men and porters. Major Guy Ward got together a parallel party of gunners to pick up batteries for their radios. Captain Dain screened the sortie with smoke shells and discouraged Chinese intervention by an occasional salvo of shrapnel. By nine o'clock all had safely scrambled back, heavily laden.

Through the morning and afternoon came several reports about the progress of the relief column. They were not encouraging: Chinese forces were said to be blocking the southern entrance to the hill road. Tanks of the 8th Hussars were sent to help them but in the afternoon the news was that the latter had lost its leading troops in an ambush. The tank carcases were blocking the road in a gorge. But this was not all. The brigadier came on the radio to say that the unrestricted passage of the Chinese past the Glosters would lead to the remainder of the 3rd Division, including the 29th Brigade, fighting to the east, being cut off from their withdrawal route. Though unlikely now to be reinforced on 25 April, it was essential for the Glosters to remain in position.

The colonel had been studying his map as he listened to this statement. When Brigadier Brodie had finished he put his map on top of the radio and replied.

"I understand the position quite clearly," he said. "What I must make clear to you is that my command is no longer an effective fighting force. If it is required that we shall stay here, in spite of this, we shall continue to hold. But I wish to make known the nature of my position."

It was a plain statement of fact. The numbers in the position capable of fighting were about 350, many of whom were wounded. A lot of weapons had been smashed. There had been no resupply of ammunition since the 22nd. Radio batteries might last a further twelve to fifteen hours. Once darkness fell, the battalion had no means of stopping the enemy from using the road below.

The brigadier recognized this but stressed that by remaining in position the battalion must pose a threat to the Chinese. They would be obliged to keep attacking and thus retain forces close to the Imjin which would otherwise be used to the south against division and corps.

Seen from the view of the commander of the 1st United States Corps, Lieutenant-General Frank W. Milburn, it was essential for the battalion to remain. This did not ease Colonel Carne's difficulties of holding fast against a third night of attacks. Yet with a calm face he set off up the hillside to the topmost ridge to consider night positions while the adjutant settled arrangements for emergency resupply by Auster aircraft and a full supply by Fairchild Packets the next day. There would be no helicopter for the wounded that night, but perhaps that also might manage to reach the Glosters' hill next morning. For the moment, a night battle had to be reckoned with: dawn on the 25th was twelve hours distant.

The remainder of the afternoon passed. Colonel Carne arranged to draw in his force tightly round spot height 235, the centre of the feature: on the north-west, "A" Company; to the east, "D" Company; south, "B" and "C"; south-west, Support Company now grouped together under their commander, Major Sam Weller. Battalion headquarters was to be sited between "A" and Support Companies. At dusk, when the Chinese could no longer see their movement, the Glosters moved together, carrying their wounded among them.

The ridge was generally bare apart from patches of sere dwarf oak and a copse of scrubby trees. The ground was rocky; tools were few. But none doubted the need to dig and, where this was impracticable, rock sangars were raised. By 20.00 hours all was quiet.

It was a time for contemplation among the defence. Some of those awaiting the enemy attack were fearful and all were apprehensive of a series of desperate battles ahead. Yet there were no signs of panic or recrimination; none of despair. A sense of determination to fight the battle out successfully was manifest. It was a mood which owed a good deal to individual valour but stemmed, too, from the immense confidence all felt in their commanding officer. He had been amongst them a good deal that day, making the occasional, quiet remark as he was apt to do, neither purveying false confidence nor betraying fears. He gave the impression of being unshakeable and they believed that he was.

By the night of the 24th/25th, according to Chinese prisoners-of-war, the 188 Division had lost over 4,000 killed and wounded since it had cross the Imjin. 189 Division began to cross the river at dusk with orders to clear away the Glosters once and for all. Commanders of the leading regiment had crossed earlier in the day to study the ground and plan the night attack. It was to begin quite silently, the assault companies creeping forward to a range at which they might effectively throw grenades – say, twenty-five yards. So six companies marched from their assembly area behind the Castle Site to the foot of Hill 235 as soon as it was dark and began stealthily its ascent.

The Glosters had put out trip wires with tins to rattle. These warnings revealed the enemy's approach at 20.45 and within a few minutes the faithful guns of 45 Field Regiment were firing into the densely packed enemy. Even so, several hundred Chinese got right up to the Glosters' defences, blowing trumpets and whistles, calling commands shrilly as they sought to overwhelm their dogged foes. Gradually, they were driven back until 23.00 hours when all became quiet once more. The Glosters set aside their dead in hollows and sent back the wounded to Captain Bob Hickey in his makeshift RAP.

Three hours later, the Chinese returned. Again the guns, the rifles and machine-guns fired, grenades were exchanged, the battle swayed to and fro. Towards dawn fresh numbers began an ascent across the little valley to the east with many trumpets directing them.

83

"It will be a long time before I want to hear a cavalry trumpet playing after this," said the colonel to the adjutant.

"It would serve them right, sir," said the adjutant, "if we confused them by playing our own bugles. I wonder which direction they'd go if they heard Defaulters played!"

"Have we got a bugle up here?" asked the colonel. The adjutant called down the question to Drum-Major Buss on the eastern slope.

"Got one in my haversack," came the reply.

"Well, play it, Drum-Major," said the adjutant.

"What shall it be, sir?"

"It's getting towards daylight; play Reveille — the Long and the Short. And play Fire call — in fact, play all the calls of the day as far as Retreat, but don't play that!"

There were a few preliminary "peeps" from the Drum-Major as he tried out his lips and then his calls rang in the morning air: Reveille, Defaulters, Cookhouse, Officers Dress for Dinner, Orderly NCOs and many more. When the last sweet note died away there was silence. Certainly surprised, perhaps confused and apprehensive of a counter-attack, the Chinese stopped their movement for a while.

The attacks began again after dawn, principally from the north, assault after assault. "A" Company were driven back from their position, being reduced to one officer, CSM Gallagher and twenty-seven soldiers. The adjutant took them back in a counter-attack and remained to command. He asked the guns of 54 Field to fire deliberately on the restored company position when a Chinese assault flowed into it. This ejected them but they massed again. The forward observation officer with the company, Captain Ronnie Washbrook, brought in with great skill a series of air strikes using napalm against those on the northern slopes. It was a joy to the defenders to see six more pairs of F 80s attack concentrations of troops from Hill 235 to the Imjin. Daunted at last, the Chinese drew back. It was 6.10 on the morning of 25 April.

The morning news came from brigade headquarters. Pressure on the route to the east had become so great that all forces were falling back towards Uijongbu. There were no troops availabe to fight a way forward to the Glosters. The battalion was to fight its own way back, given maximum support from the guns. Orders were passed to Major Weller, the adjutant, Captain Harvey, Lieutenant Temple representing Major Harding, Henry Cabral, Major Ward of 70 Battery and Captain Wisbey of the heavy mortar troop. Captain Hickey was present from the RAP. After pointing out the route to be taken and giving orders for tactical movement, the colonel paused and looked at the doctor.

"Bob, I'm afraid we shall have to leave the wounded behind."

"Very well, sir. I understand our position."

Ten o'clock was to be the hour of disengagement from Hill 235. In each defensive location beforehand, every thing of value was destroyed, to prevent it falling to the Chinese. At 10, the colonel met the adjutant.

"Let Sam Weller know that I have just been told by the brigadier that the guns are unable to support us – the gun lines are under attack themselves. Our orders are quite simple; every man to make his own way back."

Word was hastily passed: soon officers and men were hurrying down the hillside in the warm sunlight. The adjutant passed the RAP. "Come on, Bob," he called to the doctor. "The colonel will be off in a moment and that will be the lot."

"I can't go," he said. "I must stay with the wounded."

Soon none of the battalion was left on Hill 235 but the dead, the wounded and the gallant RAP staff, Padre Sam Davies amongst them.

The long ridge two miles to the south of Gloster Hill was held in strength by the Chinese and thus blocked the attempts of the Glosters to break out. Some of those running and marching away were shot down and some were captured by the enemy sallying down from the hilltops or advancing to occupy the abandoned hill.

A group under Captain Harvey took fortuitously a route first north and then west and some of this number survived a hail of fire to reach friendly lines (a total of forty-six all ranks).

By the evening of the 25th, about 350 of the battalion and its supporting Arms were being marched north across the Imjin River as prisoners of war. So too were the 63 CCF Army which had been so mauled that its remnants were withdrawn over the river to recover.

At brigade headquarters, Brigadier Brodie had written in the operations log his own documentary: "No one but the Glosters could have done it."

So passed Lieutenant-Colonel Carne's battalion of the 28th/61st Foot from view — at least for a time. But almost at once a new battalion came into being. The remaining fragment of the Glosters was ordered to the rear until a decision could be taken as to the future. This disposal reckoned without the character of Major D. B. A. Grist who had assumed command. He gathered in every officer and soldier, including those who had just escaped from the line, returned from leave or arrived from the reinforcement camp and formed them into a fighting body. Replying to a special message of encouragement from the Colonel-in-Chief, he signalled, ". . . we are already operational again." Thus continuity was maintained. As it happened, the main battle was fast waning: the Chinese strength was insufficient to carry the battle across the Han and CCF units north of Seoul began to draw back on 30 April.

From 26 April to 23 May, the Glosters with the remainder of the 29th Brigade were deployed on the Kimpo Peninsula, watching the right flank of the UN line. It was a quiet sector and here all units were reinforced and equipped anew. Major Grist was promoted to lieutenant-colonel and confirmed in command of the battalion. Officers, warrant officers and NCOs of the regiment came from far and wide to fill out the companies; many had hastened to return of their own volition as soon as they heard the news of the battalion's loss. Comrades old and new shared a unique occasion when, on 8 May, General James van Fleet, presented a Distinguished Unit Citation to the battalion and "C" troop, 170 Heavy Mortar Battery, by command of the President of the United States.

In the last week of May, once more at full strength, the British brigade returned to the Imjin, the Glosters holding the reserve position but taking an active part in patrolling north of the river. Those who had been there before were happy to see tons of defence stores arrive. The front was covered with wire; trenches were properly revetted and covered. In the August, the battalion moved forward from reserve into many of their old positions and, finally, in September, to a sector north of the river where a new line, "Wyoming", was dug and wired. From its place in this sector, the battalion was relieved by 1st Battalion, The Welsh Regiment, in November 1951.

A year and a month after leaving, the 28th/61st returned to England. Despite the pleasure of being safely at home once more, the thoughts of many of its members were often with those left behind in the prison camps.

Two main columns of British prisoners had been formed up at the end of April from those captured out of the British 29th Brigade. Amongst them were a few members of the United States Air Force shot down in the same battle area. As they marched, certain individuals and small groups escaped but the majority were secured effectively by the Chinese guards as the columns marched nightly in stages of twelve–fifteen miles until a point was reached beyond the range of day-fighter/ground attack aircraft of the United Nations. Thereafter the marches were made by day. Some of the prisoners were passed over to the North Koreans for intelligence interrogation at the notorious "Pak's Palace" at Pyongyang, in which conditions were so bad that hundreds of UN prisoners died. The majority were marched to Chiangsong on the Yalu river where a dull life was not enlivened by daily political lectures aimed at subverting the loyalties of United Nations prisoners.

In the officers' camp, Colonel Carne was singled out for prolonged isolation and beatings due to his immense prestige. Many of his officers and soldiers were also confined and beaten, and some were tortured for escape or defiance of Chinese demands for information. Less than one per cent of the British prisoners co-operated with their captors against their own country or fellow prisoners.

With the failure of their offensive in the spring of 1951, the Chinese had abandoned the hope of driving the United Nations Forces from Korea. Their problem was how to end a war which they saw they could not win, and which was unduly expensive in war material, without sacrificing all political prospect for the communist camp. Armistice negotiations dragged on from May 1951 until August 1953. Only then, at last, were the prisoners-of-war able to move south to be exchanged at Panmunjon, close to the 38th Parallel. Amongst the whole body of prisoners originally taken, many had died of neglect or starvation. Among the thirty-three dead of the Glosters' group none had died more honourably than Lieutenant Terry Waters, attacked to the 28th/61st from the West Yorkshire Regiment, who had chosen to die of his wounds rather than make progaganda broadcasts against his own nation.[1]

In the autumn of 1953, what remained of Colonel Carne's battalion sailed back into Southampton water. Sirens and hooters sounded as they came ashore to be reunited with wives and families. They were astonished and a little embarrassed to find themselves famous as men who had made history. Such is the way of the British soldier: may it always be so.

[1] Lieutenant Waters was posthumously awarded the George Cross.

Chapter Five

SIEGE AT
PRINCES GATE

Jon E. Lewis

T he Special Air Service of the British Army burst into the
world headlines in May 1980 when it stormed the Iranian
Embassy in London to free twenty-six hostages held by Arab
gunmen. It was an unusually public appearance for the SAS,
most of whose operations since its foundation in 1941 have been
deep behind enemy lines, or in the more shadowy areas of
counter-revolutionary warfare.

The man most reponsible for the foundation of the SAS was
David Stirling, a young and junior officer of the Scots Guards
who tricked his way into the British Army Middle East HQ in
Cairo in 1941 in an effort to talk to the Chief of Staff about "a
matter of operational importance". He ended up in the office of
the deputy Chief, Major-General Neil Ritche, who, impressed
with Stirling's audacity, gave him a hearing. The subaltern's idea
was to destroy Axis aircraft in the desert while they were on the
ground, using a small mobile land unit. Ritche gave the scheme
his approval and L Detachment, Special Air Service Brigade was
born. (There was in fact no "Brigade"; it was a bluff to fool
German intelligence into thinking that the unit was larger than it
was, namely a handful of men, three tents and one three-ton
truck). The badge of the SAS, the Sword Of Damocles and
wings, with the motto "Who Dares Wins", was formally
approved in 1942. Most of L Detachment's initial troopers
were disbanded commandos who, under Stirling's training and
leadership and in close liaison with the Long Range Desert
Group, proved to be formidable desert raiders. In January 1943

the 1st Special Air Service Regiment was formally recognized, and three months later the 2nd SAS Regiment was formed. In the same year, Stirling himself was captured by the Germans in Tunisia. After Africa, the regiments fought in Italy and north-west Europe. With the war's end the SAS, along with several other "private armies", was disbanded.

In 1947, however, it was reformed as 21 SAS, with a Malayan Scouts (SAS) unit coming into being in 1950. As its name implied, its chief purpose was to fight in the jungles of Malaya against the communist insurgency. The scouts were officially recognized as the 22nd SAS in 1952. Since that time, 22 SAS has been involved in campaigns in Borneo, Aden, and Oman. Following the massacre of Israeli athletes at the Munich Olympics in 1972, its counter-revolutionary warfare training and role was stepped up considerably, with the Regiment playing an active, if covert, part in the war against the Provisional IRA in Ireland and mainland Britain. It has also worked alongside the CRW units of other nations, including the West German GSG9 at Mogadishu. It therefore went in to break the siege of the Iranian Embassy at Princes Gate in 1980, the story of which is related below, with a wealth of CRW experience.

At 11.25 am on the morning of Wednesday 30 April 1980, the tranquillity of Princes Gate, in London's leafy Kensington district, was shattered as six gunmen wearing shamags over their faces sprayed the outside of No. 16 with machine gun fire and stormed through the entrance. The leading gunman made straight for an astonished police constable standing in the foyer, Trevor Lock of the Diplomatic Protection Group, while the rest, shouting and waving their machine pistols, rounded up the other occupants of the building.

The gunmen – Faisal, Hassan, Shai, Makki, Ali and Salim – were members of Mohieddin al Nasser Martyr Group, an Arab group seeking the liberation of Khuzestan from Ayatollah Khomeini's Iran. No. 16 was the Iranian Embassy in Britain. The siege of Princes Gate had begun.

A specially trained Army Commando well armed about to enter the Iranian Embassy via the first floor balcony

The police were on the scene almost immediately, alerted by an emergency signal by Trevor Lock, and were soon followed by Scotland Yard specialist units including C13, the anti-terrorist squad, and D11, the elite blue beret marksmen. The building was surrounded, and Scotland Yard hastily began putting in motion its siege negotiation machinery.

While no siege is ever the same as the one before or after it, most follow a definite pattern: in stage one, the authorities try to pacify the gunmen (usually with such provisions as cigarettes and food), and allow the release of ideological statements; in stage two, the hostage-takers drop their original demands, and begin negotiating their own escape; stage three is the resolution.

The Princes Gate siege moved very quickly to stage one, with Salim, the head Arab gunman announcing his demands over the telephone just after 2.35 pm: autonomy and human rights for the people of Khuzestan, and the release of 91 Arab prisoners held in Iranian jails. If his demands were not met he would blow up the Embassy, hostages and all, at noon the following day.

The SAS meanwhile had been alerted about the siege within minutes of its start. Dusty Gray, an ex-SAS sergeant now a Metropolitan Police dog handler, telephoned the Officers' Mess at Bradbury Lines, the SAS's HQ next to the River Wye in Hereford, and said that the SAS would probably be required at the Iranian Embassy, where gunmen had taken over. That night SAS troopers left for London in Range Rovers, arriving at a holding area in Regent's Park Barracks in the early hours of Thursday morning. The official authority from the Ministry of Defence approving the move of the SAS teams to London arrived at Bradbury Lines some hours after they had already left.

Over the next few days the Metropolitan Police continued their "softly, softly" negotiating approach, while

THE FRENCH FOREIGN LEGION: NOT MEN, BUT DEVILS

'They're not men, but devils' was the comment of a Mexican colonel afer his 2000-strong force attacked 65 soldiers of the French Foreign Legion at Camerone, Mexico, in 1863. After holding out in a ruined mud-and-brick farmhouse for eleven hours, and inflicting some 300 casualties on the Mexicans, there were just five Legionnaires still standing. With no ammunition left, the five Legionnaires fixed bayonets – and charged the encircling Mexicans. This valiant act is commemorated by the Legion every 20th April in the Fete De Camerone, the most important day in the Legion's calendar. At the Legion's HQ in Aubagne, France, there is a parade, where the history of the battle is read out and a sacred relic – the wooden hand of the Legion's commanding officer at Camerone, Captain Danjou – is held before the assembly. Afterwards bonfires are lit and Legion marching songs sung. The inspiration of Camerone is such that the Legion does not consider retreat a military option.

trying to determine exactly how many hostages were in the Embassy and where they were located. Scotland Yard's technical squad, C7, installed microphones in the chimney and walls of No. 16, covering the noise by faking Gas Board repairs at neighbouring Enismore Gardens. Gradually it became clear that there were about twenty-five hostages (as they discovered at the end of the siege, the exact count was twenty-six), most of them Iranian embassy workers. Also hostage were PC Trevor Lock and two BBC sound engineers, Sim Harris and Chris Cramer. The latter, who became seriously ill with a stomach disorder, was released by the gunmen as an act of good faith. It was a bad mistake by the Arab revolutionaries: a debriefing of Cramer gave the SAS vital information about the situation inside the Embassy as they planned and trained in a new holding area only streets away from Princes Gate itself.

Inside the holding area a scale model of the Embassy had been constructed to familiarize the SAS troopers with the layout of the building they would assault if the police negotiations were to break down. Such training and preparation was nothing new. At the Bradbury Lines HQ, SAS Counter-Revolutionary Warfare teams use a Close-Quarter Battle house for experience of small arms fire in confined spaces. (One exercise involves troopers sitting amongst dummy "terrorists" while others storm in and riddle the dummies with live rounds.)

As the police negotiating team located in a forward base at No. 25 Princes Gate (of all places, the Royal School of Needlework) anticipated, the gunmen very quickly dropped their original demands. By late evening on the second day of the siege, the gunmen were requesting mediation of the siege by Arab ambassadors – and a safe passage out of the country. The British Government, under Margaret Thatcher, refused to countenance the request. To the anger of the gunmen, BBC radio news made no mention of their changed demands, the broadcast of which had been a concession agreed earlier in the day. Finally, the demands were transmitted – but the BBC got the details wrong.

For some tense moments on Saturday, the third day of the siege, it looked as though the furious Salim would start shooting. The crisis was only averted when the police promised that the BBC would put out the demands accurately that evening. The nine o'clock news duly transmitted them as its first item. The gunmen were jubilant. As they congratulated themselves, however, an SAS reconnaissance team on the roof was discovering a way into No. 16 via an improperly locked skylight. Next door, at No. 18, the Ethiopian Embassy, bricks were being removed from the dividing wall, leaving only plaster for an assault team to break through.

On Sunday 4 May, it began to look as though all the SAS preparation would be for nothing. The tension inside the Embassy had palpably slackened, and the negotiations seemed to be getting somewhere. The gunmen's demands were lessening all the time. Arab ambassadors had agreed to attend a meeting of their COBRA committee in order to decide who would mediate in the siege.

And then, on the morning of Bank Holiday Monday, 5 May, the situation worsened rapidly. Just after dawn the gunmen woke the hostages in a frustrated and nervous state. Bizarrely, Salim, who thought he had heard noises in the night, sent PC Lock to scout the building, to see whether it had been infiltrated. The hostages in Room 9 heard him report to Salim that there was nobody in the Embassy but themselves. Conversations among the gunmen indicated that they increasingly believed they had little chance of escape. At 11.00 am Salim discovered an enormous bulge in the wall separating the Iranian Embassy from the Ethiopian Embassy. Extremely agitated, he moved the male hostages into the telex room at the front of the building on the second floor. Forty minutes later, PC Lock and Sim Harris appeared on the first-floor balcony and informed the police negotiator that their captors would start killing hostages if news of the Arab mediators was not forthcoming immediately. The police played for time, saying that there would be an update on the midday BBC news. The bulletin, however, only served to anger Salim, announcing as it did that the meeting between COBRA and the Arab ambassadors had failed to agree on the question of who would mediate. Incensed, Salim grabbed the telephone link to the police, and announced: "You have run out of time. There will be no more talking. Bring the ambassador to the phone or I will kill a hostage in forty-five minutes."

Outside, in the police forward post, the minutes ticked away with no news from the COBRA meeting, the last negotiating chip of the police. Forty-two minutes, forty-three minutes . . . The telephone rang. It was Trevor Lock to say that the gunmen had taken a hostage, the Iranian Press Attaché, and were tying him to the stairs. They were going to kill him. Salim came on to the phone shouting that the police had deceived him. At precisely 1.45 pm the distinct sound of three shots was heard from inside the embassy.

The news of the shooting was immediately forwarded to the SAS teams waiting at their holding area. They would be used after all. Operation Nimrod – the relief of the Embassy – was on. The men checked and cleaned their weapons, 9 mm Browning HP automatic pistols and Heckler & Koch ("Hockler") MP5A3 submachine guns. The MP5, a favourite SAS weapon, first came to prominence when a German GSG9 unit used it to storm the hijacked airliner at Mogadishu. It can fire up to 650 rpm. The order for the assault teams to move into place was shortly forthcoming.

At 6.50 pm, with tension mounting, the gunmen announced their demands again, with the codicil that a hostage would be shot every forty-five minutes until their demands were met. Another burst of shots was heard. The door of the Embassy opened, and a body was flung down the steps. (The body belonged to the Press Attaché shot earlier in the day. The new burst of shots was a scare tactic.) The police phoned into the Embassy's first floor, where the telephone link with the gunmen was situated. They seemed to cave in to Salim's demands, assuring him that they were not tricking him, and that a bus would be arriving in minutes to take the gunmen to Heathrow Airport, from where they would fly to the Middle East. But by talking on the phone Salim had signalled his wherabouts to the SAS teams who had taken up their start positions on the roof, and in the two buildings either side of No. 16, the Ethiopian Embassy and the Royal College of Physicians. At around this time, formal responsibility — via a handwritten note — passed from the Metropolitan Police to the SAS.

Suddenly, as the world watched Princes Gate on TV, black-clad men wearing respirators appeared on the front balconies and placed "frame-charges" against the armoured-glass window. There was an enormous explosion. The time was exactly 7.23 pm. At the back of the building and on the roof, the assault teams heard the order "Go. Go. Go." Less than twelve minutes had elapsed since the body of the Press Attaché had appeared on the Embassy steps.

The assault on the building came from three sides, with the main assault from the rear, where three pairs of troopers abseiled down from the roof. One of the first party accidentally swung his foot through an upper storey window, thereby alerting Salim to their line of assault. The pair dropped to the ground and prepared to fight their way in, while another pair landed on the balcony, broke the window and threw in stun grenades. A third pair also abseiled down, but one of them became entangled in the ropes, which meant that the rear assault could not use frame charges to blow-in the bullet proof glass. Instead a call sign from a rear troop in the garden sledge-hammered the French windows open, with the troopers swarming into the building on the ground floor. They "negotiated" a gunman in the front hall, cleared the cellars, and then raced upwards to the second floor and the telex room, where the male hostages were held by three gunmen. Meanwhile the pair who had come in through the rear first floor balcony encountered PC Lock grappling with Salim, the head gunman, who had been about to fire at an SAS trooper at the window, and shot the gunman dead.

Almost simultaneous with the rear assault, the frontal assault group stormed over the balcony on the first floor, lobbing in stun grenades through the window broken by their frame charges. Amid gushing smoke they entered and also moved towards the telex room. Another SAS team broke into the building through the plaster division left after the bricks had been removed from the wall with the Ethiopian Embassy.

Outside, at the front, the SAS shot CS gas cartridges into an upstairs room where one of the gunmen was believed to be hiding. This room caught fire, the flames spreading quickly to other rooms. (The trooper caught in the abseil rope suffered burns at this point, but was then cut free and rejoined the assault.)

The SAS converged at the telex room, as planned. The gunmen had started shooting the hostages. The Assistant Press Attaché was shot and killed, and the Chargé d'Affaires wounded before the SAS broke in. By then the gunmen were lying on the floor, trying in the smoke and noise to pass themselves off as hostages. What then happened is the subject of some dispute, but the outcome was that the SAS shot two of the gunmen dead. Afterwards, some of the hostages said that the gunmen tried to give themselves up, but were killed anyway. In the event, only one gunman escaped with his life, the one guarding the women in Room 9. The women refused to identify him as a terrorist, and he was handed over to the police. After a brief assembly at No. 14 for emotional congratulations from Home Secretary William Whitelaw, the SAS teams sped away in rented Avis vans. Behind them the Embassy was a blaze of fire and smoke.

The breaking of the siege had taken just seventeen minutes. Of the twenty hostages in the building at the time of the SAS assault, nineteen were brought out alive. The SAS suffered no casualties. Although mistakes were made in the assault (part of the main assault went in via a room which contained no gunmen and was blocked off from the rest of the Embassy), the speed, daring, and adaptability of the SAS assault proved the regiment an elite amongst the counter-revolutionary forces of the world.

Chapter Six

THE BULL OF
SCAPA FLOW

Wolfgang Frank

The Second World War was barely six weeks old when, on
13 October 1939, the German submarine Unterseeboot-
47 penetrated the British naval base at Scapa Flow, sinking the
battleship Royal Oak. It was an audacious blow, one made all
the sweeter for the Kriegsmarine in that Scapa Flow had been the
site of the scuttling of its High Seas Fleet in 1918. The crew of U-
47 returned home to Wilhelmshaven national heroes.

Günther Prien, the commander of U-47, was a natural U-boat
ace and had already claimed the first U-boat victory of the war, a
cargo ship on 5 September. An ardent Nazi, Prien had been an
unemployed merchant seaman before volunteering for the U-boat
arm (all German submarine crew were volunteers) in 1938. He had
been appointed commander of U-47 just before the outbreak of war.

After the success of the Scapa Flow raid, U-47 was sent to the
North Atlantic where it wreaked havoc amongst Allied shipping.
A type VIIIB submarine, U-47 was armed with an 8.8 cm deck
gun, a 2 cm anti-aircraft gun and five torpedo tubes (one stern,
four in the bows). Its crew was forty-four strong. Most of its
attacking was done at night, on the surface, with the deck gun,
since torpedoes were expensive and the boat could only remain
underwater for short periods.

The following account of the illustrious career of U-47,
including the Scapa Flow raid, is by Wolfgang Frank, the press
officer for the U-boat arm during the 1939–45 conflict. He both
knew most of the U-boat aces personally and occasionally
accompanied them on their voyages.

The Bull of Scapa Flow

It is worth pointing out that the most important consequence of the Scapa Flow raid was that it enabled the head of the U-boat arm, Captain Karl Dönitz, to persuade the Führer — hitherto uninterested in naval matters — to endorse a massive U-boat building programme. As Dönitz realized, single U-boat raids, though spectacular and morale-sapping for the enemy, would not greatly influence the war effort: large numbers of U-boats, organized in flotillas, or "Wolf Packs", to strangle the sea-lanes to Britain could. By the war's end some 600 submarines of the same type as U-47 had been built.

In September 1939, one of the "canoes" operating east of the Orkneys found herself off the Pentland Firth, the passage between Scotland and the Orkneys. A strong westerly current caught the boat and swept her through the turbulent narrows. Finding that his engines were not powerful enough to pull him free, the captain, making a virtue out of necessity, carefully surveyed the movement of ships and the defences in the area. On his return he made a detailed report to Dönitz, who at once saw the possibilities of a special operation. After much deliberation he ordered one of his best young officers, Lieut. Günther Prien, to report on board the depot-ship *Weichsel* at Kiel.

As Prien entered the Commodore's cabin he found Dönitz in conference with his own flotilla-commander and Lieut. Wellner, the captain of the "canoe". Charts lay spread on the table before them and Prien's eye was immediately caught by the words "Scapa Flow". The Commodore addressed him.

"Do you think that a determined CO could take his boat into Scapa Flow and attack the ships there? Don't answer now, but let me have your reply by Tuesday. The decision rests entirely with you, and without prejudice to yourself." It was then Sunday. Prien saluted and withdrew, his heart beating fast. He went straight to his quarters and settled down to a thorough study of the problem. He worked away hour after hour, calculating, figuring, checking and re-checking. On the appointed day he stood once again before the Commodore.

101

"Yes or no?" — "Yes, Sir." A pause. "Have you thought it all out? Have you thought of Emsmann and Henning who tried the same thing in the First World War and never came back?" — "Yes, Sir." — "Then get your boat ready."

The crew could make no sense of the preparations for their next patrol. Why were they disembarking part of their food supplies and taking so little fuel and fresh water with them? Apart from giving essential orders, the captain was uncommunicative, and on the appointed day the U-boat slipped quietly through the Kiel Canal into the North Sea. The nights were dark, the seas running high. While on passage the crew watched their captain closely; although funnel-smoke was sighted several times he never attempted to attack. At last, early in the morning of 13 October, the Orkneys were in sight. Prien gave the order to dive and when the U-boat was resting easily on the sea-bed, he ordered all hands to muster forward. "Tomorrow we go into Scapa Flow," he began, and went on talking quietly, making sure that every man knew what he had to do. Then he ordered every available man off watch to turn in; they would need all their strength when the time came.

At four o'clock in the afternoon the boat came to life again and the cook served a specially good meal. Jokes were bandied about and Prien wrote in his log, "the morale of the ship's company is superb." At seven-fifteen all hands went to diving-stations, and the chief engineer began to lift the boat off the bottom; the ballast-pumps sang and the boat began to move as the motors stirred into life. Prien took a first cautious glimpse through the periscope. All clear. He gave the order to surface. The wind had dropped but the sky was covered with light clouds; although there was a new moon, the Northern Lights made the night almost as bright as day.

As they moved into the narrows a powerful rip-tide suddenly caught the boat, just as Prien had expected. He needed every ounce of concentration now and a good deal of luck. The rudder was swung from port to starboard and back again, with full use of diesel engines, to keep the bows steady against the stream. At one moment he had to go full astern to avoid colliding with a blockship. Then he suddenly bent down and shouted through the hatch, "We are inside Scapa Flow!"[1]

At this point his log read, "I could see nothing to the south, so turned away along the coast to the north. There I sighted two battleships and beyond them some destroyers at anchor. No cruisers. I decided to attack the big ships." As the U-boat crept closer still, he could make out the details of the ships. The nearest to him was of the *Royal Oak* class. He went closer, until the bows of the second ship appeared beyond the first. She looked like the *Repulse*. He gave his orders, "Ready all tubes! Stand by to fire a salvo from Nos. 1 to 4!" Endrass, his first lieutenant, was taking aim; the forecastle of the *Repulse*[2] came into the cross-wires. "Fire!" He pressed the firing key.

The U-boat shuddered as the torpedoes leaped away. There was a moment's agonizing pause. Would they hit? Then a tall column of water reared against *Repulse*'s side. But *Royal Oak* lay motionless as before. A miss? Impossible. Defective torpedo? Unlikely. Minutes went by but the silence of the bay remained unbroken. Had the ships been abandoned? Was the whole of Scapa still asleep? Why no counter-attack from the destroyers? It is almost impossible to believe what happened next. Calmly deciding to make a second attack, the captain took his boat in a wide circle round the anchorage *on the surface*, while the spare torpedoes were being loaded into the tubes. For nearly twenty

[1] The entry into Scapa Flow was made through Kirk Sound, which was inadequately blocked.

[2] Prien mistook the old seaplane-carrier *Pegasus* for *Repulse*, which was not in Scapa Flow. Only *Royal Oak* was hit in both attacks. For the next five months the Home Fleet had to use remote anchorages on the west coast of Scotland, until the defences of Scapa had been put in order.

minutes he cruised round the main base of the British fleet while down below the sweating hands pushed torpedo after torpedo into place. As though the situation were not tense enough already, Prien suddenly noticed one of his junior officers, Sub-Lieutenant von Varendorff, calmly walking round the deck. "Are you crazy?" hissed the captain. "Come up here at once!" Once again Prien moved to the attack – this time at closer range – and once again the torpedoes raced towards their target.

Thunderous explosions shook the area. Huge columns of smoke and water towered into the air while the sky was filled with falling wreckage – whole gun-turrets and strips of armourplating weighing tons apiece. The harbour sprang to life. Morse signals flashed from every corner, searchlights probed and swept, a car on the coast road stopped, turned and flashed its headlights on and off as though signalling, as it dashed back the way it had come.

"Emergency full ahead both!" ordered Prien. "Group up motors. Give me everything you've got!" As the water bubbled and boiled beneath the U-boat's stern, he saw a destroyer coming swiftly towards him, sweeping the water with her searchlight. She began to signal with her Aldis lamp; Prien bit his lip as the bridge beneath him shuddered to the vibration of the screws. His wake showed up all too clearly yet he could not afford to reduce speed. Suddenly the miracle happened; the destroyer dropped astern, turned away and disappeared. A moment later he heard the crash of her depth-charges in the distance. The U-boat scraped past the end of a jetty and then – "We're through! Pass the word, we're through!" A roar of cheers answered him from below. Prien set course for the south-east – and home.

During the long hours of waiting before the attack, the crew had passed round a comic paper; one of the cartoons in it showed a bull with head down and nostrils smoking. "Harry Hotspur," someone had said; that was also their name for their captain. Now, on the way home, Endrass had an idea. Armed with paint-brushes and some white paint a small working party clambered on to the casing and painted on the side of the conning-tower the boat's new crest – the Bull of Scapa Flow.

While crossing the North Sea they listened to the wireless. "According to a British Admiralty report," said the announcer, "the battleship *Royal Oak* has been sunk, apparently by a U-boat. British reports say that the U-boat was also sunk." The men in *U-47* smiled. In the afternoon came an official announcement from the German Admiralty: "The U-boat which sank the British battleship *Royal Oak* is now known to have also hit the battleship *Repulse* and to have put her out of action. It can now be announced that this U-boat was commanded by Lieutenant Prien." For the first time the name of Prien was heard by the German people. Prien in Scapa Flow – where twenty years before, the German High Seas Fleet had gone to the bottom!

As the U-boat made fast to the jetty Dönitz could be seen standing next to Grand Admiral Raeder, the corn-flower-blue lapels of his uniform clearly visible. The Grand Admiral came on board to congratulate the crew; offering his hand to each man he conferred upon every one of them the Iron Cross, Second Class, while the captain was awarded the First Class of the Order. "Lieutenant Prien," said Admiral Raeder, "you will have an opportunity of making a personal report to the Führer." Turning to Dönitz he then announced before them all that the Commodore had been promoted to Rear-Admiral. Henceforth he would be the Flag Officer Commanding U-boats. That same afternoon Prien and his crew were flown to Berlin. Hitler received them in the Reich Chancellery and conferred upon the captain the Knight's Cross of the Iron Cross.

In June, 1940 *U-47* was patrolling to the west of Scotland, still commanded by Lieut. Prien, the "Bull of Scapa Flow". The weather was calm and mild, the nights so light that one could read a book on the bridge at midnight.

SAS SELECTION

Colloquially known as 'the Sickeners', the selection tests for the British Special Air Service (SAS) are amongst the toughest for any elite force. The Selection Training Course, based on one designed by Major John Woodhouse in 1950, places the emphasis on both physical and mental strength. Candidates begin with road runs and proceed to a number of rigorous cross-country marches carrying bergen rucksacks weighing up to 25kg. The culmination of the Selection Training Course is 'The Fan Dance', a 60km land navigation over the Brecon Beacons in South Wales which has to be completed in 20 hours regardless of weather. By this stage a third of the candidates will have dropped out or been 'binned'. But this is not the end of the selection process – candidates stil have to endure seven weeks of Continuation Training, which includes simulated interrogation by enemy intelligence forces, a five day 'escape and evasion' test, where candidates have to live off the land equipped only with a knife and a box of matches, and parachute training. Successful Candidates are then finally admitted to 'the Regiment'.

Early one morning the haze lifted to reveal a ship – their first target for days. Just as *U-47* altered course to attack, the target turned too and came straight down at her. Prien lowered his periscope and dived as fast as he could to 180 feet, while the ship rumbled unwittingly overhead. Almost at once he surfaced again, ordering the gun's crew to their stations; but as they were closing up round the gun, an after look-out suddenly reported more smoke astern of the U-boat and Prien realized that a convoy was approaching. He abandoned his original plan and, after sending out a hasty sighting-report to head-quarters, he submerged again.

As soon as *U-47* was running smoothly at periscope-depth, he took a quick look through the lens as it broke surface for a few seconds. He could hardly believe his eyes. Forty-two ships were steaming majestically towards him in open order, seven columns of six ships of all shapes and sizes, escorted by two ancient-looking destroyers and three modern ones. For three hours, still submerged, Prien tried to close on the convoy, but his boat was too slow; steadily he lost bearing on the ships, until they were out of periscope sight. He started to surface but almost immediately a trawler hove in sight and he had to dive; at his next attempt a Sunderland zoomed out of the sun like a fat bumble-bee and forced him below again. Prien now realized that to catch up with that convoy he would have to chase it for at least ten hours, and by then it would be so close to the coast that he would never get near it for aircraft and surface-escorts. As he sat weighing up his chances and scanning the horizon, masts and smoke suddenly appeared to port and a straggler from the convoy came hurrying along, zigzagging violently. So he stayed below the surface, and everyone kept deathly still, as if the U-boat herself were holding her breath like a living thing. "All tubes ready!" Every man was standing tensely at his post. Suddenly the ship turned away; with a curse Prien called for the last ounce of power from his motors as he stood after his prey. "No. 5, stand by . . . fire!" Some seconds later there was a clanging crash. "We've hit her near the funnel!" called Prien triumphantly. "She's the *Balmoral Wood*[1] — look and see how big she is, I'd put her at 5,000 or 6,000 tons." As the water closed over the sinking ship, all that could be seen on the surface were a few large crates, some of which had burst open to reveal aircraft wings

[1] This ship was torpedoed and sunk on 14 June 1940.

The first U-boat capture of the war when the damaged U-570 surrendered to a Hudson on 28th August 1942. Seen here entering a British port.

and fuselages. "Well, *they* won't be dropping any bombs on Kiel, anyway," commented one of the crew.

All next day Prien carried out a searching sweep on various courses, but sighted nothing. "The Atlantic seems to have been swept clean," he wrote in his log. But his luck changed with the dawn of the following day, for a 5,000-tonner without lights came steaming past, barely 5,000 yards away. Despite the growing daylight, Prien tried to approach on the surface but he was soon forced under by a Sunderland; however, he was determined to get in an attack and once again he surfaced. This time his first hasty look round revealed warships ahead and merchant ships astern of him; quickly he sent out a sighting signal and dived again, realizing that he had chanced upon the meeting-place of a convoy with its escort. He moved in to attack but soon saw that the twenty ships in convoy were screened by at least four escorts of the *Auckland* and *Bittern* class, while a Sunderland flew above them. His original plan of attack would be of no avail against such a strong escort, so he waited awhile before surfacing and then made a wide sweep round, so as to try his luck from the other side. As night fell he closed in, once more at periscope-depth, and began to look for a likely target. The weather was favourable; white caps of foam on the waves would make it difficult for the enemy look-outs to spot his periscope, and although the sky was cloudy, visibility was good.

Despite all this, it looked as though the U-boat had in fact been sighted, for one of the escorts turned towards *U-47* and came down like a pointer sniffing into the wind for game. The range dropped quickly — 300 yards, 250, 200 . . . Prien was tempted to fire at the escort, but she suddenly turned away and disappeared on a course parallel to the U-boat. With a sigh of relief Prien ordered, "No. 1 ready . . . fire!" His target was a great tanker, deeply laden, which had caught his eye earlier in the day. He did not wait to see the torpedo hit, but turned immediately to his next victim, which was slightly nearer — a ship of about 7,000 tons. "No. 2 . . . fire!" While the U-boat was still heeling, Prien suddenly saw a column of water spouting up alongside a ship he had not aimed at. There had been a slight mishap in the torpedo compartment; the torpedo-artificer had been thrown off his balance by the movement of the boat and had saved himself from falling by catching hold of the firing-grip. As a result No. 3 tube had fired a fraction after No. 2 – but the torpedo had hit a second tanker.

Fifteen minutes later the U-boat surfaced and Prien sprang up to the bridge; it was not yet quite dark and the sea was getting up. Over on the port quarter lay the big tanker with a heavy list, her bows well below the surface, her decks awash. Prien sent for the silhouette-book and soon identified the battered wreck as that of the tanker *Cadillac*, 12,100 tons.[1] The other ship, of which nothing could now be seen, was presumably one of the *Gracia* class of 5,600 tons. The third had also disappeared. Now for the rest of them!

But it was not to be; a storm blew up and after two days' fruitless search Prien realised that he had lost the convoy. A day later, however, he sighted and sank the Dutch tanker *Leticia*,[2] 2,800 tons, bound for England from Curaçao with fuel-oil. Late that night, in a freshening sea, yet another tanker was sighted and Prien ordered the gun to be manned, having decided to stop the ship with a couple of well-placed rounds and then sink her at his leisure. "Only five rounds of ammunition left, Sir," warned the coxswain. – "Never mind, we'll use them just the same." Time passed but there was no sign of the captain of the gun. Prien called down the hatchway, "Control room! Where's Meier?" There was the sound of running feet below, then the voice of the control room petty officer. "Meier is lying in his bunk, Sir, and says there's absolutely no point in trying to aim a gun in this weather." Prien could hardly believe his ears; the bridge watch did their best to hide their amusement. "Give him a

[1] Probably the tanker *San Fernando*, torpedoed and sunk on 21 June 1940.
[2] Sunk on 27 June 1940.

direct order from the captain to report immediately on the bridge!" When Meier at last appeared he did not trouble to hide his feelings. "In *this* sea, with only a couple of rounds?" − "They *must* hit, Meier!" − "Aye, aye, Sir." Indifferently he moved towards the gun and Prien gave the order to open fire. The tanker turned sharply away as the first shells screamed towards her, but two of them hit her; Meier was excelling himself. "Hit her in the engine-room!" ordered Prien. Another hit − but the target was still moving away. The last of the five rounds went into the breech, and this time the shell-burst was followed by a cloud of grey smoke and a yellow flash. Soaked to the skin, Meier returned to the bridge; the tanker had stopped and the crew were hastily abandoning ship. Throwing a quick word of congratulation to his still impenitent gunner, Prien brought *U-47* into a good firing position and loosed off a torpedo. His log reads: "The torpedo hit and the ship began to sink. Despite the gunfire and the torpedo-hit, her radio operator continued to signal '*Empire Toucan* torpedoed in position 49°20' North, 13°52' West' and later 'Sinking rapidly by stern'. Finally he jumped overboard with a flare and was seen swimming away from the ship." Prien immediately steered towards the flare but when he reached the spot, there was nothing to be seen. A brave man had died. . .

Weeks went by as Prien and his brother captains hunted and sank, watched and waited, shadowed the convoys and "homed" other boats on to them, in fair weather and in foul. When at length the U-boats returned to France for repairs and provisioning, their crews were sent to the new rest-centres at Carnac and Quiberon near Lorient, where they could relax on the beach, bathe, ride and do exactly as they pleased. Here they could let the world go by, as they took the pretty daughters of France by storm and quaffed the local wines; all too soon they would once more be at sea, the perpetual thunder of the diesels around them and the waves foaming and crashing on their decks.

Prien, too, was soon back at sea. One dark and rainy night, he and half a dozen other boats encountered a convoy, which they attacked from all sides at once. This was one of the earliest organized wolf-pack actions of the war, and will go down in history as the "Night of the Long Knives". Torpedo after torpedo raced from its tube to detonate against some ship's side. Ten thousand tons of petrol went up in a fiery ball of white-hot flame a thousand feet high; an ammunition ship exploded with a deafening roar and literally disintegrated; all around was nothing but the bright glow of flames. Some ships stood on end before finally disappearing, some listed heavily and turned turtle, others broke apart, to die a painful death. Everywhere, like a pack of wolves, the U-boats were at the convoy. With all his torpedoes gone, Prien reckoned up the tonnage he had sunk by identifying his victims from the "picture book". Then he took a signal-pad and wrote, "Have sunk eight ships in the convoy totalling 50,500 tons. All torpedoes fired."

The dawn came slowly, marking the end of the "Night of the Long Knives". The other commanders were also making their reckoning: Kretschmer, Schepke, Frauenheim, Endrass, Bleichrodt, Moehle and Liebe. In two days of operating together they had achieved the staggering figure of 325,000 tons sunk.[1] Within a few days U-47 had returned to her base. Prien, as the first U-boat captain to top the 200,000-ton mark, now became the fifth officer in the armed forces to receive what was then the highest decoration – the Oak Leaves to the Knight's Cross.

Afterword

The luck of U-47 ran out on 8 March 1941, when it was sunk by HMS Wolverine, with the loss of all hands. During its career the boat had sunk 28 ships totalling 160,939 tons.

[1] "Night of the Long Knives" – 18/19 October 1940.

Chapter Seven

THE EAGLES OF BASTOGNE

Laurence Critchell

In December 1944, Hitler threw twenty-four divisions into a final desperate offensive against the advancing Allied armies on the Western Front. The Führer's plan called for a breakthrough in the Ardennes which would split the Allied armies in two, and allow the Wehrmacht to push on to the port of Antwerp. The offensive took Eisenhower and his commanders by surprise and initially the Germans made signficant progress, causing a "bulge" in the front line. It became vital that the Allies held the Belgian town of Bastogne, situated astride a major north-south, east-west crossroads, and the US 101st Airborne Division was committed to the town's defence. Nicknamed "The Screaming Eagles", the 101st was made up of numerous component units, but principally the 501st Parachute Regiment, the 502nd, the 506th, the airborne artillery, and the 327th Glider Infantry — in total some 11,000 men. Now temporarily under the command of Brigadier-General Anthony McAuliffe (both usual division commanders were in the US), the 101st drove through the night from Northern France in 380 trucks on 17 December, travelling with headlights on in a calculated risk to gain time, reaching Bastogne in well under twenty-four hours. This account of the town's defence by the 101st is by Laurence Critchell, then a line office with the division, and begins with the 101st arriving at Bastogne on the 18th, where they met straggling groups of US soldiers in retreat and an overwhelmingly larger German force poised to encircle the town completely. Already honoured for their part in the D-Day landings, the 101st found their greatest test was about to begin.

SAS and Elite Forces

It was foggy and damp at six o'clock in the morning. The 1st Battalion had been selected to lead off on the push out the Longvilly road. The coatless men moved through the streets of Bastogne, sloshing in mud and dirty water. Between their double lines, on the road itself, heavy armor still was moving eastward, away from the oncoming enemy. It was a ludicrous sight to see a few of the airborne troops wave at the retreating armor — fire power much stronger than any of them could have. One paratrooper, still without a weapon, picked up a stick and, for the benefit of the demoralized columns, shook it in the direction of the enemy. Here and there unhelmeted men were wearing wool caps or were bareheaded. Few wore overcoats. But they pushed forward out of the town with a sense of confidence, and in a little while they were in the silent, foggy countryside.

Following the 1st Battalion as it moved out of Bastogne was B Battery of the 81st Anti-Aircraft with eight 57-mm guns. Behind that unit in turn — considerably behind it, as a matter of fact — were the 2nd and 3rd Battalions of the 501st. The latter was getting itself badly tangled in the snarl of traffic within the town, and since Ewell was not yet certain of how and where he would employ those battalions, he contented himself with the advance of the 1st Battalion and its supporting unit along the Longvilly road. On one occasion the men turned off by mistake towards Marvie, due east. But Ewell was able to set them right, and by 07.30 in the morning, with the light just breaking, the situation looked fair enough.

In that region the Bastogne-Longvilly highway ran along a valley dominated on each side by gently sloping hills. Those hills were partially covered with sparse vegetation, but the overgrowth offered little concealment. On this morning, however, the fog was dense. It was so thick that the left flank guards of the 1st Battalion by-passed two platoons of enemy infantrymen dug in on a hill in the vicinity of Bizory; though slight sounds carried distinctly on the damp air, neither the Germans nor the Americans became aware of each other's presence. Unsuspecting, the 1st Battalion marched straight towards the main body of the enemy.

The Germans, of course, were equally unsuspecting. Until that moment they had forced back the stubborn 28th Division, and the less stubborn, badly fragmented 9th Armored Division, without meeting heavily organized resistance. This had given the ordinary German soldiers new confidence; their morale was higher on the morning of December 19th than it had been since the invasion of the Normandy coast. In documents and letters taken from German prisoners or from German dead, the enemy soldiers were writing home, "At last the war has become fun again."[1] They described the slaughter of armored and infantry divisions along the way as "a glorious blood bath" and prophesied to their families in the clean little towns of Germany that the European struggle would soon be at an end. Once again, evidently, it was *Deutschland über Alles*.

The first encounter with the deployed 1st Battalion of the 501st Parachute Infantry in the early hours of 19 December must have been a shock to them.

Contact was made at what seemed to be an enemy road block near the village of Neffe. The division reconnaissance platoon, which had somehow gone astray at the beginning of the advance, was on the point of overtaking the lead scouts of the battalion when, from the fog directly ahead, there was the unmistakable fast rattle of a German machine-gun.

Almost to a man, the battalion went flat. With the first sounds of fire the two German platoons which had been by-passed in the fog discovered their enemy in front and behind them. The confusion was so great that the German

---

[1] From a document taken by a 501st prisoner of war interrogation team.

guns were quickly disposed of. However, the machine-gun that had opened up at the crossroads and given the first alarm of the Bastogne siege, evidently outposted a lead element of considerable weight.

The valley road at that point did not pass through the center of the valley, but ran close to the rising ground on the left flank. Thus it was only on the right, where the valley sloped away to a small stream, that it was possible to deploy the men adequately. In keeping with McAuliffe's words, Ewell drily told the commander of the 1st Battalion, Lieutenant Colonel (then Major) Bottomly to "develop the situation." He himself found a stone house in a pocket of the hillside and established a temporary command post. Within a short time Bottomly reported to Ewell by radio that he was opposed to approximately two platoons of infantry and two Mark IV tanks. Ewell, to whom the report was put in the form of a question, told him to go ahead and fight his own fight.

The Mark IV tanks were firing, from a defiladed position near Neffe, straight down the highway. Consequently, the 57-mm guns of the anti-aircraft company could not be brought to bear on them. And by ten o'clock in the morning, with no advance having been made on either side, the situation became a deadlock. Little more could be done just then; in Bastogne the 2nd and 3rd battalions still were struggling to get through the choked traffic of the VIII Corps, fleeing to the rear.

Off on the left flank of Ewell's position was a group of large farm houses in a broad valley. The valley ran down towards Neffe, but before it reached that village (held, Ewell judged, by the enemy) the ground rose up again to conceal the two villages from sight of each other. It occurred to Ewell that if the 2nd Battalion were to seize the town of Bizory, which lay in that direction, his men would be well situated to move onto the high ground adjacent.

Lieutenant Colonel Homan was in command of the 2nd Battalion. Implementing Colonel Ewell's orders as soon as he got free of Bastogne, he seized Bizory with no opposition and only a little fire from the direction of the deadlock at Neffe. During this time the 3rd Battalion, still in Bastogne, was trying to get out of town by an auxiliary side route. Ewell ordered the commander, Lieutenant Colonel Griswold, to strike for Mont, farther to the right of the forward positions then held by Bottomly and Homan. Ewell eventually intended to use Griswold's battalion in a flanking attack on Neffe, but he kept these intentions to himself. What chiefly concerned him was getting the battalion out of town.

Bastogne at that hour still was crowded with drifting and staring men. So great was the shock they had received that many of them were inarticulate. They trickled through the German lines in two and threes, making no attempt to organize themselves, refusing to be organized by anyone else. When they asked the paratroopers what they were doing, and the paratroopers replied, "Fighting Germans," they only stared. To them, at least temporarily, the war seemed lost.

Not all were like that, however. Some of the haggard, beaten men accepted a K ration, ate it silently, and then asked for a rifle. They were ready to go back and fight. Some of the armor was in good shape, and the morale of the armored men who elected to remain at Bastogne and fight it out was high. Among them, seven tanks and three tank destroyer crews organized themselves into a combat team and voluntarily attached themselves to the 2nd Battalion, while another platoon of armored infantry stuck it out with the regiment until the siege was lifted.

By noon of the 19th the situation was clearer. The 1st Battalion was halted at Neffe, fighting what Ewell thought was only a difficult road block. The 2nd Battalion had seized Bizory and was deployed on favorable high ground. The 3rd Battalion had reached Mont, but because the ground

---

JAGDVERBAND 44

Formed by Generalleutnant Adolf Galland in February 1945, the Jagdverband 44 unit of the Luftwaffe was arguably the greatest concentration of flying talent ever witnessed. Its pilots included Gerhard Barkhorn (302 victories), Johannes Steinhoff (176 victories), and Walter Krupinski (197 victories). The unit's formidability was only added to by the fact that it flew the revolutionary Me262 jet, which had a maximum speed of 870km/h in level flight – far outclassing any Allied plane.

---

between there and Neffe was flat, and the enemy fire heavy, the soldiers had been unable to carry out the second phase of the order and sweep down on the road block at Neffe. By these three operations, however, a line had been stretched along commanding ground outside of Bastogne to the northeast. This was the critical and – as events later proved – decisive deployment.

Ewell decided to move his 2nd Battalion to Magaret, which would still further improve their position. He sent Colonel Homan with one company of men to secure the approaches to that town by seizing a small patch of woods on a long ridge above it. Homan did so, but was presently engaged along his entire front.

Company I had been separated from the 3rd Battalion and was making a reconnaissance of wooded areas to the front. It was ordered into the town of Wardin to investigate the reported existence there of an armored road block. The ill-fated company encountered the enemy in the town, but at 15.00 radioed that its men were doing all right. When a company of volunteer tank destroyers arrived at Ewell's command post, however, he sent them to the 3rd Battalion to help out in case the group at Wardin needed support.

It was then 16.00. Ewell had formed three battalions approximately abreast and in contact with the enemy all along his front. For the first time since the German break-through, the enemy was meeting a line of troops which refused to give ground.

At dark Ewell ordered the battalions to break contact and form to defend a general line along the high ground to the west of Bizory-Neffe and roughly parallel to this line to the southward. Taking his plan back to the red stone buildings where division headquarters had been established, he got McAuliffe's approval. On the way he assured himself, for the first time since daybreak, that Bastogne had not been seized.

Walking along the main street of the town, he met a sergeant of Company I.

"Have you heard about Company I?" asked the sergeant. "It's been wiped out."

Ewell, hurrying back to his radio, didn't believe it.

The town of Wardin lay on the extreme right flank of the Bizory-Neffe-Wardin line, which Ewell had formed on the commanding terrain northeast of Bastogne. Wardin was a small place of a dozen-odd houses, set at a little distance from one of the main roads entering Bastogne. Captain Wallace had taken his men of Company I into the village as part of the general reconnaissance ordered by Homan in compliance with Ewell's instructions. What ensued there was tragic.

When Wallace and his men entered the town, they encountered only a few Germans. Without much diffi-culty, they drove those men from the dreary Belgian houses and took possession. Wardin had strategic value and, though it was closer to the enemy than Bizory and Neffe, Wallace believed he could hold his place.

He and his men had been in the town only a short while, however, when a force of German armor appeared unex-pectedly on the outskirts. As the tanks – they were Tiger

Royals — spread out to prevent Wallace's force from escaping, the tank gunners opened fire point-blank. Under cover of this fire, a whole battalion of German infantrymen, who had all the ardor of their late successes, closed in to the streets. Wallace hastily withdrew part of his force to fight at the flanks of his command post and to keep one avenue of retreat open. The remainder of the Americans held out in the concealment of the houses.

The din was soon terrific — the fast rocketing *"whisht-bang!"* of heavy-caliber shells at close range, the clattering of fallen rock, the explosions of bazooka shells, the rattle of small arms and the queer vibrating *"brrrrrrrp!"* of German automatic pistols. Bazooka gunners deliberately squatted in the open where they were plainly visible to the Germans and fired point-blank on the tanks. Soldiers in the houses held their positions until shells burst through the rooms and demolished the lower floors. Other soldiers snatched up the bazookas of men who had died.

House by house, fighing in a blaze of fire, the Americans retreated. The smoke of explosions from the tank guns clouded vision from one side of the street to the other. The Germans were systematically demolishing every house. Everywhere was the ammoniac stink of cordite; in the rubble of the demolished buildings hands, heads, legs protruded. Those paratroopers who still were alive fought their way towards Wallace and the command post. One youngster running out into the center of the street, deliberately knelt in a furious rattle of small-arms fire and discharged a bazooka shell squarely into the lead tank. The tank was halted and, though the boy was dead an instant later, the rest of the oncoming armor was momentarily canalized.

Wallace, giving the infantryman's equivalent of "abandon ship," ordered the remainder of the men to split up — to get back to Bastogne singly or in pairs — any way they could.

On the street before the command post the men threw up a hasty tank obstacle. As the armor and the swarms of German infantrymen approached this final point, Wallace directed all the fire power at his disposal to cover the withdrawal of the men who were left. One by one, as the small-arms and heavy-caliber fire grew heavier, they passed through the barricade, Wallace urging them on. Then the officer ordered the men at the barricade, too, to fall back. A few of them refused. The final survivors of the trap of Wardin saw, as they looked back, the figure of their captain, still at the barricade, still fighting — the last they were ever to see of him.

All that afternoon and night the survivors trickled into Bastogne. At the regimental command post, a great room which had once been a school study hall was set aside for them, where they cleaned their weapons on the children's desks. They were very silent. A few of them sat against the wall, under a statue of the Crucifixion, with their heads in their hands.

Wallace, like many of his men, left a wife and child behind him. Of approximately 200 of his soldiers who had gone into Wardin eighty-three survived.

Undertones of tragedy marked the evening of the first day at Bastogne. As the light dimmed in the sky, the streets of town became deserted. The inhabitants disappeared into their cellars. In the great dark rooms of the regimental command post the only illumination came from the flicker of the squad cookers as the survivors of Company I heated their K rations. Nothing had been heard of a truck column bringing ammunition and other supplies to the town. Father Sampson was missing. And there were rumors that our division hospital, set up to the rear of Bastogne, had been captured.

The 501st Command Post was plainly visible from the enemy lines. With the exception of the church across the street, it was the most prominent building in Bastogne. Downstairs on the main floor were a dining hall, and immense cloister with Doric columns, a skylight, and an adjacent chapel. The chapel was used for a temporary aid station, while the cloister was designated for use by the company and regimental kitchens (if the equipment got through). The dining room, which occupied a wing of its own, was left to the Franciscan nuns, who were taking care of twenty or thirty very young, very curious children. It was interesting to note that, when the German artillery began to fall on Bastogne, those children disappeared underground with the nuns and did not reappear until three weeks later.

Upstairs in the seminary were dozens of connecting rooms, each of them piously decorated. Above the second floor were dormitories for the former pupils, while on the fourth floor was a vast chamber which had been occupied before the Ardennes break-through by VIII Corps military police. The haste with which the MPs had abandoned their quarters was evident in the discarded material strewn about the floors: paper-bound books, magazines, pin-ups, ga-loshes, webbing, blankets, even uniforms. The few of us who explored this room felt a little satisfaction in the debacle of the withdrawal — mute testimony of that upheaval of life which had come to a rear echelon when it had suddenly become a forward area.

By morning of the next day, 20 December, the tempera-ture had dropped below freezing. There was little wind before dawn, and the unmoving blanket of clouds limited visibility in the darkness. The 501st men were in the same positions they had taken up at nightfall and not much had been done to extend the flanks. Though other units had been brought up to either side, the 501st still was squarely in the line of the German advance.

One of the first moves made by McAuliffe, as an artillery commander, was to dispose his airborne artillery and tank guns in such a manner as to bring coordinated fire from all

US NAVY SEALS

Taking their name from the three elements in which they were trained to fight (sea, air, land), the US Navy SEALs were amongst the most effective American special forces in Vietnam. Inserted by boat into the Mekong delta swamps, camouflaged 'search and destroy' SEAL teams spearheaded The Phoenix Program which succeeded in reducing Viet Cong strength in the delta from around 80,000 to 20,000 personnel. SEALs in Vietnam also worked in conjunction with attack-trained dolphins. As many as 60 enemy frogmen may have been killed by these dolphins.

of the pieces on any one point of the line which he intended to "develop", or which was attacked by the enemy. Subsequently, when Bastogne was encircled, he was able to deliver the same concentration of fire on any point of the 360° defense. On the morning of the 20th, however, his main concern was the sector occupied by Ewell's regiment. And the honors of the day were about evenly divided between Ewell's men and McAuliffe's artillery.

The night had been reasonably quiet. From the Americans captured at Wardin the Germans had identified the division opposing them, and they evidently spent the hours of darkness massing their forces for a major drive. The much criticized G-2 of the Allied armies at the time of the Ardennes break-through was not the only one to be surprised in those days; documents later captured from the German staff revealed the enemy's astonishment of finding the 101st Airborne Division (which their intelligence had reported to be at Mourmelon, France) directly in the path of their advance at a key focal point of communications, a hundred miles from where they were supposed to be.

The first troubles on the 20th began at 05.30, before there was light in the wintry sky.

East of Bizory, where Homan's 2nd Battalion men were deployed, was a rise of high ground. Between that high ground and the American front line was a clear field of fire, extending more than 3,000 yards. On that expanse, the only cover for an attacking enemy was the natural defilades where the farmland rose and fell. Homan's position was ideal for defense – so ideal, as a matter of fact, that, when an observation-post spotter who had field glasses reported that six enemy tanks were starting across the fields, accompanied by what he estimated to be a battalion of German infantrymen, the event took place at such a distance that the Americans, though alerted, could only sit by their guns and wait.

A scratch force of American tank destroyers had attached itself to Homan's battalion during the night. At word of the impending attack, the crews disposed their vehicles north of the village of Bizory on either side of a small road that was a key approach to the American lines. Meanwhile, Homan had notified Ewell about the approaching enemy; Ewell had notified Kinnard, and Kinnard, through McAuliffe, the artillery. One by one the guns within Bastogne were brought to bear on a predetermined coordinate – where, when the signal came to fire, their shells would drop in a screen across the oncoming Germans.

The expanse of ground in front of Homan was so great that the Germans advanced for a whole hour before they were close to the coordinate for the artillery barrage. During part of this time the men of the 2nd Battalion could keep them in sight, and, the nearer they approached, the brighter grew the morning. When the American machine gunners suddenly opened fire, the tank destroyers fired simultaneously, and, within an instant or two, in a curtain of artillery bursts, the German lines were struck squarely by hundreds of shells from McAuliffe's guns.

From full silence to the blaze of fire took only a few moments. The Germans still were at such a distance from Homan's men that the automatic weapons' fire had little visible effect. But so intense was the coordinated artillery fire from within Bastogne that the paratroopers, who had a grandstand view of the entire episode, witnessed the Germans begin to falter. Here and there, among the mushrooming clouds of artillery smoke, the tiny black figures stumbled and fell. Behind them one of the heavy tanks turned back towards its own lines — then rolled and halted. Two of the tanks were destroyed, and a third disabled.

The tiny figures of the Germans began to run. More and more of them fell. For twenty minutes the rolling barrage continued to pursue them. When it lifted, the only Germans who remained on the open fields were the scores of still bodies.

The shock of that first repulse must have been a severe one to the German troops. Until that morning they had met other pockets of stubborn resistance — the 7th Armored Division, whose soldiers had made a gallant stand at St. Vith, and the elements of the 28th Division already mentioned. But when the Germans, filled with confidence, attacked Bastogne on the morning of the 20th, they were repulsed not only with heavy casualties, but also by a group of organized soldiers who obviously intended to deny — to twenty-five enemy divisions — a critical road-net in the heart of the salient.

Towards midmorning of the 20th it started to snow. The German forces, under cover of thick woods to the northeast, began to shell Bastogne, devoting particular attention to the huge building by the church steeple.

This was the building which we had selected for a regimental command post. It was the largest command post any regiment could have had. It was five stories high and perhaps a quarter of a mile in circumference. The walls were about three feet thick. This was thick enough to withstand shellfire, but unfortunately, the operations offices had been selected in the very first hours, before anyone knew the direction of the enemy. When the lines were consolidated outside Bastogne, it was found that the Germans could – with good luck in their marksmanship – put artillery through the windows.

The snow came down steadily, gently. Soon it blanketed the bodies of the dead Germans at Neffe and those beyond Homan's positions outside of Bizory. The paratroopers were seeing the last bare earth they were to see for two months. Meanwhile, the shelling of Bastogne continued. The Germans regrouped for a concerted attack in force, and the fateful day was quiet.

The 1st Battalion, which had fired the first shots of the Bastogne siege, had been unable to seize Neffe beyond the turn of the valley road. Company B had successfully taken a house on the side of the critical Neffe road, and, from the windows of that house, the soldiers were able to command all the approaches to the battalion front. Machine guns were set up in there, while the infantrymen of the other companies dug foxholes and, where they could, lined the interiors with straw.

In Homan's area at Bizory, where the first enemy attack in force had been repulsed, there was no change. But at Griswold's 3rd Battalion, which had taken up positions at Mont, the 1st Platoon of Company B of the 705th Tank Destroyer Battalion had attached itself during the night. This was a valuable reinforcement. Griswold posted one of the vehicles at a bend in the Neffe road, where it commanded the stretch leading to that enemy-occupied town, and where it also commanded a draw leading off to the south. Another destroyer was placed to complement the fire of the first, while the second section of the platoon, from concealed positions, guarded the approach directly across the valley.

Everywhere there was silence. The skies were leaden; the snow came down steadily, almost audibly. No planes were in the air anywhere. At division headquarters, McAuliffe, in contact with General Middleton by radio, happened to remark that Bastogne would probably be surrounded.

The soldiers blew on their stiffening fingers and waited.

At seven o'clock a few shells fell in Bizory and Mont. These were followed by a few more and, shortly, by a great number. Finally, a heavy barrage dropped on all the critical points along the defensive line. So intense was the artillery fire from the German positions that within a few minutes every telephone wire connecting the battalions to regimental headquarters was severed.

When the firing slackened off, the German forces struck simultaneously in a two-pronged offensive against the 1st and 3rd battalions.

Bottomly, and the 1st Battalion, radioed Ewell that the enemy troops were charging straight down the highway. They came with the shouts and high morale of men convinced they were going through. Not even in Normandy had the paratroopers encountered such high morale. Bottomly reported to Ewell that it was too dark to see much, but that he could hear tanks coming along with the troops.

It was a bad hour for the regimental staff at Bastogne. On orders from someone, the records were packed, the equipment readied, the men dressed for retreat. If the two flanks collapsed . . .

The snow had ceased. The night was bitter cold.

There were eleven battalions of guns at McAuliffe's disposal within Bastogne. All eleven battalions dropped a

127

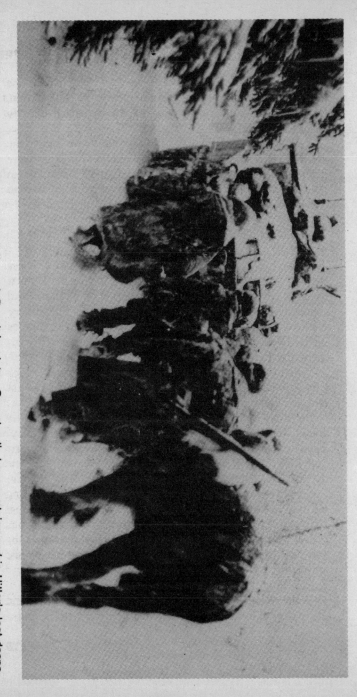

The Second World War was fought all out through Russia's winter, Greenland's icy mountains and in Hitler's last desperate gamble in the Ardennes 1944.

"dam of fire" across the Neffe road, approximately 200 yards ahead of the town. It was the most effective American defensive fire during the siege. Three German tanks — two Panthers and a Tiger Royal — were struck almost at once; they had drawn up beyond the last houses in the village when they were hit, and there they stayed.

The short delay before the artillery barrage, however, had enabled a considerable number of German infantrymen to approach so close to the American lines that the greater number of shells fell behind them. Those men charged wildly towards the Americans, firing and shouting. Company B, posted in and around the house, on commanding ground at the side of the road, took the shock without yielding an inch of ground. The automatic weapons in the windows controlled the approaches so effectively that not a single German soldier got within bayonet distance of the American lines. Everywhere in the darkness the enemy troops stiffened and fell and died, and their blood spotted the snow. Weeks afterward they were still there, grotesque and stiff, the foremost bodies 300 yards in advance of the wrecked German armor.

The action in this area continued with intensity for some time. The soldiers were fighting in that bitter fume of smoke and sweat and cold where each man seemed hopelessly alone. There was no consciousness of cold or snow or wet clothes or hunger. When men are fighting each other, and the issue remains in doubt, there are only the simplest and most basic elements of human experience.

Meanwhile, the men of the 3rd Battalion were struggling to hold back a simultaneous enemy attack from a different quarter. It was evident that the Germans had abandoned their attempt to enter Bastogne across the wide field of fire opening down from Homan's positions, where they had failed that morning. The dual attack by dark left Homan's forces alone and evidently had the object of bending the two flanks of the 501st until those flanks collapsed and Homan was trapped in the middle.

The Germans attacking Griswold's forces also had supporting armor. But the enemy tank commander must have observed the tank destroyers behind the American lines, for his armor did not leave the concealment of a little wood just west of a château at Neffe. From that position the tanks could put down a base of fire for their advancing and – as events shortly proved – suicidal infantrymen.

The open and comparatively smooth slope which separated Mont and Neffe afforded a field of fire for Griswold's battalion almost as extensive as that which fronted the 2nd Battalion under Colonel Homan. In addition to this wide field of fire, the slope was crisscrossed with man-made obstacles – a checkerboard of barbed-wire fences erected by the Belgians to make feeder pens for cattle. The fences were in rows about thirty yards apart. Each fence was five or six strands high. Because of the manner of their construction, it was almost impossible to crawl underneath the fences; a man approaching Griswold's forces at Mont had to halt at each obstacle and climb through.

Whether the German commanders knew of the existence of these obstacles and decided to risk the attack anyway, or whether the leading enemy soldiers just stumbled onto them by accident in the darkness, will probably not be known. But the attack, once launched, had to be carried on. The German infantrymen ran forward with the same enthusiasm, the same wild yells and eagerness, which had characterized all their offensive actions since the breakthrough. When they reached the fences, they simply climbed through. But it broke them.

As fast as they reached the obstacles, Griswold's machine-gunners swept them down. The Germans were in great strength, and the forces behind, pressing upon the forces ahead, made a massacre inevitable. Bodies of the dead piled up around the wire fences, and the attackers who followed, climbing over those bodies, became bodies themselves a few steps beyond. The volume of tracer fire from Griswold's gunners was spectacularly intense; prisoners questioned later said that its visible effect, as much as the holocaust around the fences, was to them the terrifying element of the night attack.

What Griswold's men were facing was a whole German regiment – the 901st *Panzergrenadiers*, better soldiers than the *Volksgrenadiers* who had attacked Homan to no effect in the early morning. These Germans rushed towards the 3rd Battalion of the 501st with such high spirit that, despite the wire fences and the field of fire, Griswold was forced to regroup part of his battalion to reinforce his left flank. By the time he accomplished this, the action had become intense and the German casualties terrible. The total destruction of one side or the other was so imminent that the American tank-destroyer men, having no targets for their guns, fired the .50-caliber weapons from their vehicles, jumped out, and joined the infantrymen on the line.

By the time the German fire began to slacken off, the insane double attack of divisional strength had lasted four hours. It was close to midnight. Enemy dead were piled up in such numbers around the wire fences that even the German withdrawal was difficult. Around Neffe, where the other attack had taken place, the situation was much the same, and, though the casualties on the American side had been very heavy, the *Panzergrenadiers* had been decimated. Ewell's eye for ground had given the paratroopers an advantage they were never afterwards to lose.

As he remarked later: "I think that, as of that night, the 901st had 'had it'. They no longer had enough men to be an effective offensive force. They had been pretty well chewed up before they got to us, and we completed the job."

At the regimental command post, the staff unpacked to stay.

As everyone knows, the newspapers in the United States did not announce that the 101st Airborne Division had been cut off and surrounded by the enemy until a day or two before the relief of the besieged city. Oddly enough, most of us at Bastogne were almost as slow in getting the news.

Newspaper maps of front lines in a war usually show a salient in clear black, like a pool of spilled ink. The impression is that within that pool the land is thick with soldiers, that every square inch of terrestrial space has its allotted guardian. Nothing of the sort is true, of course. The break-through of the German tanks in Holland and their advance on Veghel through the heart of the enemy country were more typical than unique. Where the vehicles crossed the highway, and where they approached Veghel – both being guarded areas – they were engaged. But the remainder of their movements was through virtually deserted countryside, like the land on the road from Addeville to La Barquette.

Something of the sort was just as true at Bastogne. The first evidence of enemy forces to the rear of Bastogne came when a reconnaissance patrol engaged a small force of Germans on the road leading back to the hospital. In a few hours the enemy forces had moved elsewhere; but, as time passed, engagements on the roads to the rear became more frequent. McAuliffe at division headquarters knew that Bastogne would be ringed by the enemy, but at the respective regimental headquarters, and especially on the battalion lines, only rumors of the engagements to the rear reached the men. On the night of the 20th and the morning of the 21st the whole situation was in doubt. Yet the front lines of the German drive had already gone beyond Bastogne.

Von Rundstedt was aiming for Liège, where the largest supply dumps behind the Allied lines were situated. His plan was to seize those dumps and thus equip his army for the drive on Antwerp. Once Antwerp had been reached, the Allied forces would be split in half.

Nothing of this was known, however, on the morning of the 21st in Bastogne. After the Germans had fallen back, all was still and cold. The gentle descent of the snowflakes by the old church on the main street gave Bastogne the picturesque air of an old-fashioned Christmas card. By morning the snow had made the whole town clean and white – dangerously white for patrols; so Captain Phillips, with Lieutenant Frank as interpreter, ransacked the houses of Bastogne for bed sheets to use as camouflage.

That day – for the first and last time of the war – the operations offices of regimental headquarters moved underground.

A narrow corridor about ten feet below the surface of the earth, reached by a flight of stone steps, admitted to a series of cement-walled chambers underneath the convent command post. Each room was about ten by fifteen feet. When desks and chairs were put in, there was not much room to move around. The regimental commander, his executive officer, the adjutant, the intelligence officer, the operations officer, and their enlisted staffs were all crowded together into the connecting rooms. With the exception of the apartment in a private house across the street, occupied by the prisoner of war interrogation team, and with the further exception of a few aid stations, those underground chambers were the only warm rooms in Bastogne during the siege. They were not only warm, they were also safe. And consequently very crowded.

One of the last convoys to go through to Bastogne from outside brought the regimental kitchens. For lack of space in the forward positions the mobile stoves were set up – with nothing to cook – along the sides of the glass-ceiled cloister upstairs and beneath a huge statue.

The wounded who came from the lines were put temporarily in the cold chapel adjacent to the cloister. Major Carrel, the regimental surgeon, was ill, but Captain W. J. Waldmann of Bakersfield, California, a man with a high forehead and a grave manner, took his place. Operations and transfusions were performed by the yellow light of two gas lamps. The wounded men, wrapped in the few blankets on hand, were laid on the freezing floor of the chapel. As new casualties were brought from the lines, aisles were made between the litter cases. Soon the floor was covered with wounded men, who lay where they could see the crazy shadows dancing on the plasma tubes and the gas bottles for the lamps.

Presently, the enlisted men of the staff realized that no wounded were being evacuated. And that was how the word of the encirclement finally spread.

Four German divisions and elements of three others faced the 101st Airborne Divison when Bastogne was finally surrounded. Each of our men was outnumbered four to one. No one felt heroic about this, and no one made any speeches about it, written or otherwise. The troops were never called upon – as democratic statesmen are so fond of doing, especially after lunch – to give no inch of their embattled ground. Nor were they ever told that what they were doing was important, significant, or destined by any combination of circumstances to go down in military history. It was even doubtful that General McAuliffe's mimeographed Christmas message to the troops reached every foxhole.

But as soon as the word spread among the troops, both in town and on the lines, that the roads out of Bastogne had been cut off and the division surrounded, a curious, very subtle change took place in the atmosphere. It was difficult to understand. Perhaps it was this:

A certain good-natured rivalry had existed from the beginning among the various units of the division – the 501st, the 502nd, and 506th, the 327th Glider Infantry, the airborne artillery, and the others. In England, in Normandy, in Holland, in France the good-natured conviction of each unit that its own soldiers were the best had persisted. However, the various units as a whole considered themselves head and shoulders above the other divisions in the ETO.

So when Bastogne was surrounded, and the circle of the defense was manned, not by strangers, but by the "old gang" – the "Hell Raisers" of Newbury and Lambourne and Chilton Foliat and Littlecote and Greenham Common and Carentan and Eindhoven and Nijmegan – and we knew that the rear was protected and the flanks secured by what we considered the only kind of soldiers worth fighting with, the atmosphere in Bastogne became much as it would have been if someone had erected a sign on the highest point of town – HOME STATION – SCREAMING EAGLES.

No matter where the Germans attacked around the circle, the men of the other units could say to themselves: "The Five-O-Deuce is getting it right now," or "Poor Sink. He's having a bad night." They could trust the 502nd or the 506th or any of the others. Those were not regiments a self-respecting 501st man would want to join, naturally (on account of Sink or Michaelis or too much "chicken", or any one of a dozen reasons), but they were a damned sight better regiments than any others in the ETO.

The stray units and fragments of units which had stayed to fight with us were not accepted just as additional fire power. By their free decision to remain and fight they were raised to the level of the airborne troops; were given, so to speak, honorary membership in the division. There were no strangers in Bastogne during the siege. Only after the siege had been lifted, and sad-faced, weary infantrymen of the relieving units filed by the hundreds through the ruined streets, did our men, and those who had fought with us, realize what had come to us for a little while and gone, and would never come again.

The day of the 21st was quiet for our regiment. The Germans had decided to abandon the attempt to gain

Bastogne through the positions chosen by Colonel Ewell around Bizory, Mont, and Neffe, and were spreading around the town.

McAuliffe, worried by the dwindling supply of ammunition, and still in contact with higher headquarters by radio, asked for air resupply as soon as the weather cleared. He was promised it – *if* the weather cleared. But with the leaden skies over the town, as they had been closed over all of Europe almost without break since early November, there seemed little hope.

Captain Waldmann, working in the chapel hospital, knew that his supply of plasma would last only another day or two. Even by then, in spite of everything that he, Captain Axelrod, Captain Jacobs, and the other medical officers could do, some of the wounded had died. Outside in the courtyard, piled in the trailer of a jeep, were dead soldiers from the line, their bare legs, yellow in color, sticking out from under a frozen canvas cover. Everywhere, things were half-completed or not done at all. As the German shelling grew heavier and heavier, and the third night fell, the American artillerymen within the town counted their ammunition. On the lines the inadequately clothed men fought back strong, continual, probing attacks and counted their own ammunition. The situation at Bastogne that night and the morning of the 22nd was at its lowest ebb.

Around 11.30 in the morning of a dirty gray day – the 22nd – four tiny German figures waded up through the snow on the road from Remoifosse to the American lines. The soldiers of the artillery unit who had dug themselves into fortified positions along the sector drew a bead on the target. But they held their fire. The Germans were carrying a large white flag.

Word passed down through the front lines like an electric shock: the Germans wanted to surrender!

The Eagles of Bastogne

The road from Remoifosse happened to lead to Colonel Harper's medical station. There, to the astounded medics, the German group — a major, a captain, and two enlisted men — reported themselves in crude English and demanded to be taken to the commander of troops in Bastogne. Both officers were arrogant, and it annoyed them to be blindfolded. So Colonel Harper left them at his command post.

On the line many soldiers crawled out of their foxholes, stretched upright in full sight of the Germans across the way, and, for the first time since their arrival, took time to shave. Men of the other sectors were more cautious, but Colonel Harper's men knew they were safe as long as the German emissaries were inside Bastogne. So they relaxed and ate their K rations with legs dangling over the edges of foxholes.

Division headquarters had been set up above and below ground in a series of red-brick storehouses, not unlike garages, where the VIII Corps had had its own headquarters. German artillery shells had been falling on the brick houses at least once an hour. But during the presence of the German intermediaries the morning was still.

Colonel Harper and Major Jones took the surrender message to General McAuliffe. The note read as follows:

The fortune of war is changing. This time the USA forces in and near Bastogne have been encircled by strong German armored units. More German armored units have crossed the river Ourthe near Ourtheville, have taken Marche and reached St. Hubert by passing through Hompres-Libret-Tillet. Libramont is in German hands.

There is only one possibility to save the encircled USA troops from total annihilation: that is the honorable surrender of the encircled town. In order to think it over, a term of two hours will be granted beginning with the presentation of this note.

If this proposal should be rejected, one German artillery corps and six heavy AA Battalions are ready to annihilate the USA troops in and near Bastogne. The order for firing will be given immediately after this two hours' term.

All the serious civilian losses caused by this artillery fire would not correspond with the well-known American humanity.

And now let Colonel Marshall tell what happened:

McAuliffe asked someone what the paper contained and was told that it requested a surrender.

The General laughed and said, "Aw, nuts!" It really seemed funny to him at the time. He figured he was giving the Germans "one hell of a beating" and that all of his men knew it. The demand was all out of line with the existing situation.

But McAuliffe realized that some kind of reply had to be made and he sat down to think it over. Pencil in hand he sat there pondering a few minutes and then he remarked, "Well, I don't know what to tell them." He asked the staff what they thought, and Colonel Kinnard, his G-3, replied, "That first remark of yours would be hard to beat."

General McAuliffe didn't understand immediately what Kinnard was referring to. Kinnard reminded him, "You said 'Nuts!'" That drew applause all around. All members of the staff agreed with much enthusiasm and because of their approval McAuliffe decided to send that message back to the Germans.

Then he called Colonel Harper in and asked him how he would reply to the message. Harper thought for a minute but before he could compose anything, General McAuliffe gave him the paper on which he had written his one-word reply and asked, "Will you see that it's delivered?"

"I will deliver it myself," answered Harper. "It will be a lot of fun." McAuliffe told him not to go into the German lines.

Colonel Harper returned to the command post of Company F. The two Germans were standing in the wood blindfolded and under guard. Harper said, "I have the American commander's reply."

The German captain asked, "Is it written or verbal?"

"It is written," said Harper. And then he said to the German major, "I will stick it in your hand."

The German captain translated the message. The major then asked: "Is the reply negative or affirmative? If it is the latter I will negotiate further."

All of this time the Germans were acting in an upstage and patronizing manner. Colonel Harper was beginning to lose his temper. He said, "The reply is decidedly not affirmative." Then he added, "If you continue this foolish attack your losses will be tremendous." The major nodded his head.

Harper put the two officers in the jeep and took them back to the main road where the German privates were waiting with the white flag.

He then removed the blindfold and said to them, speaking through the German captain: "If you don't understand what 'nuts' means, in plain English it is the same as 'Go to Hell.' And I will tell you something else – if you continue to attack, we will kill every goddam German that tries to break into this city."

The German major and captain saluted very stiffly. The captain said, "We will kill many Americans. This is war."

"On your way, bud," said Colonel Harper.[1]

---

[1] From *Bastogne – The First Eight Days*, by Colonel S. L. A. Marshall.

The small party of the enemy, carrying their white flag, disappeared down the snowy road in the direction of their own lines. The USA troops climbed back into their fox-holes.

And the threatened artillery barrage failed to materialize.

Shortage of ammunition, especially for the artillery, was McAuliffe's chief concern. That day the 463rd Field Artillery Battalion had only 200 rounds of ammunition.

McAuliffe passed the word to ration the firing to ten rounds per gun per day. He clarified his order for one artillery commander just before an enemy attack: "If you see 400 Germans in a 100-yard area, and they have their heads up, you can fire artillery on them — but not more than two rounds."

There was food — two boxes of K rations a day per man — but not for long. And the snow was blanketing the lines deeper. Already trench foot had set in.

Not enough maps, not enough ammunition, not enough clothing, not enough plasma, not enough food . . . What *was* there enough of?

Well, there was enough spirit.

And the next morning, after a night of heavy fighting in other sectors, the miracle happened. It was a simple miracle. Yet for a continent where months of winter had already grayed the skies day after day without change and would gray them again solidly for months and months afterwards, leaving only that one small patch of good weather in the dead center of a crisis, it *was* a miracle.

For the skies cleared and the sun came out.

And up from England by the hundreds roared the C-47 supply planes and the fighters — throttles open — destination: Bastogne.

"The fortunes of war are changing . . ." It was a double-edged phrase.

The sun had not been up an hour before our first American fighter planes appeared. They were cheered by the frozen paratroopers at Mont and Bizory and Neffe and all along the lines — small silver planes which came swiftly from very high up and in a few moments were roaring in circles around the town, a thousand feet above the foxholes. Men who had gone to sleep in covered positions underground were awakened by the familiar thunderous buffeting of air pressure cause by exploding bombs. Within Bastogne the few windows still unshattered shook and rattled and subsided and then shook again.

Those men who had a good view of the German lines — like Major Pelham, who occupied an observation post in a private farmhouse clearly visible to both sides — could watch the planes dive on some object behind the German positions, then pull up in a fine curve a few hundred feet off the ground, leaving behind, where the bomb struck, a perfectly-formed balloon of orange flame and black smoke which expanded soundlessly, brilliantly, and with spectacular beauty over the dazzling, snow-white hills. Moments later the sound would come.

The noise continued all day. Between the concussions of the exploding bombs we could hear the occasional *"whiff-fisssssss!"* of rockets from the Typhoons — a sound that brought to mind, all in a piece, the golden lines at Eerde and along the Neder Rijn. Close liaison was maintained by radio with the air support around Bastogne, and one infantryman, who reported five German tanks bearing down on his position, had six P-47s darting upon the tanks within a few minutes.

Close to the red-brick buildings which housed division headquarters was a gentle slope of hillside clear of shrubbery or trees. It was concealed from the lines by a higher rise of land beyond. This bare slope, dazzling white with snow in the sun, was selected as the drop zone for the C-47 supply ships. Division S-4, Colonel Kohls, placed Captain

Matheson of the 506th and Major Butler of the 501st in charge of the bundle recovery, and notified each regiment to send five jeeps with trailers. Distribution of the parachuted supplies would be made directly from the field.

No hour had been given McAuliffe for the expected arrival of the C-47s. So from the break of dawn on a freezing crystal morning, 23 December, Butler, Matheson, and the supply officers of the other units, each with a jeep of his own, stamped their feet, blew on their fingers – and waited. The rumor of an air resupply had reached the men on the lines, and, with the Germans virtually immobilized by the daylight bombing, they were having a quiet, cheerful morning. In straw-filled foxholes, dugout command posts, and farmhouses the American soldiers waited.

The first C-47s to reach Bastogne dropped parachutists. They were pathfinders out of England – men who had been called from classes at school several days before, and who had been waiting all this time for clear weather. They landed safely, set up radar sets – refinements of those which had been used in Normandy – and guided the resupply ships to the drop zone.

At 11.50 the planes roared in – 241 of them.

What ought to be said is difficult to say. A tribute is an awkward thing. Even the men who felt like waving their arms and yelling did nothing at all except stare up in silence at the roaring planes. Bastogne vibrated with the thunder of American engines. These were the pilots, many of them, who had flown the division to the invasion of Normandy half a year before. They were the men who had been criticized or scorned by the parachutists for taking evasive action under fire – and who had then flown them to Eindhoven and Zon and Eerde and Veghel without mistake.

And now here they were again, the other half of the airborne equation, our young fellow countrymen, the youngest of all soldiers, sweeping in with their olive planes through the clear, blue December sky of Belgium, and low over the snow-covered hills, to resupply — in a town the world was watching — the same old gang.

Crowds of Belgian townspeople emerged from their catacombs under the houses to stare. It was difficult for us not to feel a sentimental pride of country. The equipment parachutes, blossoming over the white field where Butler and the other men waited to receive them, were green and blue and yellow and red — ammunition, plasma, food, gasoline, clothing . . .

The planes made a circle of the besieged town and then turned away to the north, flying at an altitude of about a thousand feet. Flak had become heavy, but not a single plane took evasive action. The controls of one ship were shot away just as it swept, empty of its parachuted supplies, over the German lines. Its pilot had been gaining altitude. As the bullets struck it, a little wisp of brown smoke gusted out in a faint streak from its tail. Slowly the plane curled upon one wing and nosed down into a vertical dive. The airborne troops who watched, and who had ridden so often in the familiar C-47 cabin, could imagine the scene inside: the two American youngsters struggling with the controls, the cockpit windows showing nothing but uprushing earth, the instinctive start backwards towards the cabin, and then . . .

A balloon of smoke and fire went up from the earth where the plane fell.

The drop zone was only a mile square. Yet ninety-five per cent of the 1,446 parachuted bundles were recovered. One hundred and forty-four tons of fresh supplies had come to Bastogne.

So speedily did the supply crews make distribution and load the bundles into jeeps (without stopping to detach the parachutes) that the artillery units were firing the new ammunition before all the bundles on the field had been recovered.

When the second aerial resupply was made, the ammunition shortage was no longer a problem. Gasoline had the lowest priority; since the division was not going anywhere, only 445 gallons were delivered. But food supplies, which had the second highest priority, remained far below the margin for safety, even after the deliveries had been made; the 26,406 K rations that had been dropped were, though impressive in figure, enough to feed the division personnel for only a little more than a day.

McAuliffe authorized foraging.

Troops like to forage, and nobody is better at it than the American soldier. An abandoned corps warehouse yielded 450 pounds of coffee, 600 pounds of sugar, and an equally large amount of Ovaltine. Most of those items were delivered to the aid stations for the use of the wounded. In an abandoned corps bakery, flour, lard, and salt were uncovered, while from a Belgian warehouse came margarine, jam and additional supplies of flour. Also found in the latter storehouse were 2,000 burlap bags. These were sent out to the front lines for the soldiers to use as padding for their feet.

The farms at the outskirts of town yielded potatoes, poultry and cattle, the staples most needed for the men. Because discipline and selflessness were at the highest during the siege, the soldiers who commandeered such items took them back to the kitchens at the regimental command post, instead of roasting or cooking them makeshift on the spot. As a result, the butchered farm animals were skinned and cleaned properly, and the meat was divided evenly among each of the battalion kitchens. It was not uncommon, in those uncommon days, to see the skinned, bloody carcass of a whole cow or a gigantic hog being hosed down by the cooks on the stone floor of the cloister at the regimental CP, under a blue and gold statue of the Virgin Mary.

Oddly enough, the cooks themselves worked under intermittent shellfire. The glass ceiling of the cloister was also the roof of the building, and shells from the German guns to the northeast sometimes burst among the stone cornices. The KPs were kept busy sweeping away the broken glass. It is a statement of fact that no place in Bastogne could be termed a rear area. After the first German bombing, the town was sometimes more dangerous than the lines.

The fighting that took place on the 23rd and 24th, in different sectors of the all-around defense, was intense. The lines of the 501st Parachute Infantry underwent continual probing attacks by the Germans, especially each nightfall, but after the first two days the Germans had clearly abandoned the costly effort to enter Bastogne over the wide fields of fire which opened from the regimental positions. Division headquarters had no such respite, however, and for every six-hour period in Bastogne there were one or more attempts by the enemy to break through in force. Those who lived within the town seldom guessed how many men were dying in the suburbs to keep the streets empty of all but Americans.

McAuliffe had conceived the expedient of drawing a small reserve from each of the organizations on the line. These reserves were formed into a task force, with armor and tank destroyers, and were used as a mobile support, capable of moving to any sector of the line seriously threatened by an enemy attack. Ewell, copying the plan, created Task Force X, under Captain Frank McKaig and Lieutenant Ernest Fisher, to support his own battalions. For some reason, the Germans never attacked simultaneously on all sectors of the perimeter defense, so the mobile task forces were an effective device.

Approximately 2,000 civilian inhabitants of Bastogne remained in the town during the siege. They lived underground in mass shelters, one beneath a convent in the center of the town, another beneath the regimental command post.

A few lived under their own houses. Those who lived in the great cellars of the two convents dwelt in conditions of indescribable filth. Old men, too crippled to move, sat in chairs at the side and stared into the darkness; young children crawled about the cement floors; men and women lay together on rough blankets or piles of burlap. At the regimental command post, this condition became such a threat to the health of the soldiers that at length certain male civilians were assigned the task of policing their own shelters and, under shellfire, of emptying the refuse outside.

An interesting, though rather ugly sidelight of life in Bastogne during the siege was the impossibility of digging slit trenches or making other arrangements for field sanitation. A large privy was dug in the courtyard outside the regimental command post, but because that area was under constant shellfire, few of the men would use it. In the beginning they utilized a large indoor latrine obviously built for school children. However, the plumbing froze after the first day; so in time the place was boarded up. From then on, at all hours of the day and night, soldiers could be found searching for unused toilets through the smaller rooms upstairs in the seminary.

The day and nights were bitter cold. Ewell authorized his men to wear whatever would keep them warm. That no loss of discipline occurred during the resultant individualism was a tribute to the discipline already ingrained in the troops. A few hours after the word had gone around, many soldiers appeared in civilian sweaters, crude blouses of parachute silk, and Belgian winter caps. One officer wore a Canadian combat jacket which he had saved from Holland. An enlisted man appeared at the command post in any army blanket, with holes cut for his arms and a rope binding it about his waist. He was the personification of the Sad Sack, but no one seeing the stubble or beard on his chin, the lines of weariness around his eyes, the tight, humorless slit of his mouth and the dirty hands cracked from exposure, gripping the one clean thing in his possession – his rifle – could have smiled.

The parachutes recovered from the equipment bundles were used to cover the wounded men. The command post personnel donated their blankets to the men on the line. Every civilian sheet and blanket in town had already been collected and put to use. Also every bottle of liquor.

On the afternoon of 23 December, word came to Bastogne that Patton's armor was fighting its way to the besieged town. If luck held, Patton – with the division commander, General Taylor, in the vanguard – would reach Bastogne by Christmas Day.

Early in the evening of 23 December, just after the winter darkness had fallen and a brilliant three-quarter moon lighted the snow-bound little town with a blue glare, Chaplain Engels, Lieutenant Peter Frank, Sergeant Schwartz and Sergeant Harvey were having a premature Christmas dinner in the second-floor apartment of the prisoner-of-war team, across the street from the regimental command post.

The chaplain had just come in from the lines, where the night was almost as quiet as it was in town. In the blacked-out, rickety apartment there were light and warmth. Lieutenant Frank, a Viennese by birth and an American by choice, had a flair for entertainment. He had set the supper table with linen, silver, wine glasses, plates, and candles – all (except the seminary candles) borrowed from the abandoned supplies of the house. Three bottles of looted wine were open on the sideboard; a stock of good Belgian cigars had been set out, and in the frying pan on the stove was steak, a gift from Chaplain Engels.

In half an hour the party had become merry and mellow. It is traditional with soldiers to feel more and more immortal as the wine is drained, and, the more immortal they feel, the more they toast each other's imminent death:

this must be the root of that brooding melancholy which characterizes so many drinking songs. The officers and men toasted one another's distant wives and sweethearts, departed friends, and one another's lives and imminent deaths; they all toasted, in the old, old manner, confusion to their enemies.

"Gentlemen," announced Lieutenant Frank, "the Queen."

Everyone rose.

"Stalin," proposed Sergeant Schwartz.

"General Ike."

Glasses clinked.

"Benes . . ."

"McAuliffe . . ."

"Lady Macbeth . . ."

When the dinner was over and cigars had been handed around, the group, with Lieutenant Frank at the piano, sang Christmas carols.

They were midway through *Silent Night* when a buffeting of air pressure shook the floors and rattled the windows.

"Somebody's getting bombed," said Frank, pausing.

"Go on, Lootenant," said Harvey, " 'sh probably Berlin."

But a moment later a soldier put his head in the door. "German planes," he announced. "They're bombing the town."

There was a little silence. Then Frank said: "The hell with it. I'm staying here."

"Of course," said the chaplain, lighting a cigar.

But the next bomb exploded with such violence that one of the windows burst inward. The floors wobbled and shook. Plaster fell. Rushing to the door, the chaplain shouted the time-honored battle-cry of the infantry school – "FOLLOW ME!" – and fell head-over-heels downstairs.

The first bombs were dropped uptown in the vicinity of a railroad overpass near division headquarters. An aid station was hit, killing most of the men and, with them, a Belgian girl who had volunteered to work as a nurse. Other bombs then struck the houses on the square below division headquarters, bracketing the group of shelters where the Belgian citizens had taken refuge and demolishing a memorial statue to the Belgian dead of World War I. One bomb had struck only fifty feet from the command post.

Another bomb tore through two floors of the command post itself and lodged – unexploded – in the ceiling of a potato cellar.

The force of aerial-bomb explosions defies description. Soldiers in Bastogne that night could tell by the rattle of anti-aircraft fire whenever the planes were coming to dive down. The small-arms fire always grew heavier as the plane reached the bomb-release point of its dive: this crescendo of noise had the same effect on the nervous system as a crescendo of drums. When the plane had swept by, the firing ceased, and then everyone knew that the bomb was on its way. Conversation ceased. Sometimes we could hear the high, whistling flutter of the descending projectile, and then death was very close.

Fires burned later in the town that night. Out on the lines, one or two of the battalion command posts had had near misses, but no one had been injured. Desolation gripped the upper regions of the town, however, and when the fires burned themselves out, only the charred skeleton of buildings remained around the main square. Bastogne, which had been untouched when the troops moved in, wore that ghastly air of desolation which had come to so many European towns in the war. In the still night a man walking past the ruins could smell the sickly-sweet odor of the untended dead.

This was Christmas, 1944.

Chapter Eight

THE SCUD-HUNTERS

John Amos

The 22nd Special Air Service Regiment came to the attention of the world in May 1980 when troopers from its B Squadron stormed the Iranian Embassy in London and, in the full glare of the TV camera, rescued 19 hostages. It was an unusually public appearance for the unit, most of whose operations before and since have been deep behind enemy lines or in the more shadowy areas of Counter-Revolutionary Warfare (CRW).

The present day 22 SAS Regiment, the direct descendant of the wartime SAS of David Stirling (see "Birth of a Legend", pp 162–69), was formed in 1952, and began its career fighting guerrillas in Malaya (since 1957, Malaysia), Borneo, Oman and Aden. In recent decades the main SAS effort has been directed against the IRA, both in Ireland and on the mainland. The Regiment — to itself it is always "the Regiment" or "Sass", never "S.A.S." — has also used its counter-terrorist capability to help other European security forces. In May 1977 it helped Dutch marines and police to deal with the hi-jack of a passenger train by South Moluccan gunmen, and five months later worked with the German GSG9 at Mogadishu. Five years on, the SAS was asked to fight a so-called "general war" in the Falklands. In 1990, the Ministry of Defence once again called on 22's special service and sent it to fight Saddam Hussein in the Gulf War. It was almost a homecoming for the Regiment, for it had been raised in the desert fifty years before. And, as the story of the 22 SAS patrol codenamed "Bravo Two Zero" shows, the intervening years had done nothing to diminish the professionalism and physical capability of the SAS trooper.

The 22nd SAS Regiment was alerted for action within hours of Saddam Hussein sending his armour rolling into oil-rich Kuwait at 0200 (local time) on 2 August 1990. At Stirling Lines, the SAS camp situated behind a nondescript 1950s red-brick housing estate on the edge of Hereford, a small batch of troopers was issued desert kit and briefed. They were flown out to Saudi Arabia later that month, carrying hand-held designators (which "paint" targets for the laser-guided bombs of Allied aircraft), as part of the United Nations' Operation "Desert Shield", the securing of the Saudi border from further Iraqi encroachment.

More teams of SAS followed. Initially, it seemed that the SAS would be employed in their role as hostage rescuers. The commander of the 40,000-strong force which made up the British contribution to the anti-Saddam Coalition, Lt-General Sir Peter de la Billiere ("DLB"), had previously fought with 22 SAS in Oman and Malaya, and commanded the Regiment during the Falklands conflict. He had also planned the 1980 seizure of the Iranian Embassy at Princes Gate. Now, in the Gulf, he was faced with another hostage situation, Saddam's use of "guests" as human shields at important military installations. Eventually, however, de la Billiere ruled an SAS mass rescue mission. The hostages were constantly moved and the intelligence inside Iraq was not good.

Meanwhile, the number of 22 SAS at the regimental holding area in Saudi Arabia grew steadily. By early January 1991 the force assembled totalled 300 badged SAS soldiers, plus 15 volunteers from the elite reserve team of the part-time Territorial Regiments, 21 and 23 SAS. It was the biggest gathering of the unit since the heady days of World War II.

For an agonising period, however, it looked as though the unit would be given no role in Operation "Desert Storm", the Allied offensive to remove the Iraqis from Kuwait. The SAS were gathered like so many racehorses before a race, but not sure if they would be allowed to run. The Commander-in-Chief of the Allied forces, US General H. Norman "Stormin' Norman" Schwarzkopf, intended to degrade Saddam's military capability by a huge air campaign, while finishing him off with a completely conventional – if tactically brilliant – infantry and armoured envelopment. Also, like many senior military figures, the irascible Schwarzkopf was no admirer of special forces. Reputedly, he had met a contingent of US Special Forces in the Gulf with the greeting: "I remember you guys from Vietnam . . . you couldn't do your jobs there, and you didn't do your job in Panama. What makes you think you can do your job here?". However, de la Billiere, the only non-American on Schwarzkopf's planning staff, CENTCOM, was determined to find a job for his old Regiment. In the second week of January, de la Billiere identified a task for 22 SAS, to cut roads and cause diversions in the enemy rear, thus pulling troops away from the front. After a presentation by the SAS themselves, Schwarzkopf gave 22 SAS the go-ahead. They would cross the Iraqi border right at the beginning of the air campaign. This was scheduled to begin on 29 January. The SAS was in the war.

As the Regiment made itself ready at its holding area, the world was hypnotised by the deadline by which President Bush insisted Iraq implement United Nations' Resolution 660 (Iraqi withdrawal from Kuwait), midnight on 16 January. Saddam refused to blink or budge.

The Regiment was as surprised as most other people when hundreds of Allied aircraft and Tomahawk Cruise missiles began bombarding targets in Iraq just before dawn on 17 January. Within twenty-four hours the Iraqi airforce was all but wiped out and Saddam's command and communications system heavily mauled. Allied commanders retired to bed at the end of D-Day most satisfied.

The only nagging area of Allied doubt was Iraq's Scud surface-to-surface (SSM) missile capability. Though an outdated technology, a Soviet version of Hitler's V2, the Scud was capable of carrying nuclear and bio-chemical warheads. It could be fired from a fixed site or from a mobile launcher. Could Saddam still fire his Scuds? Would he? On the second night of the air campaign, Saddam answered all speculations by launching Scuds (all with conventional warheads) at Saudi Arabia and Israel. The six which landed in Israel injured no one, but they were political dynamite. If Israel responded militarily the fragile coalition, which included several Arab members, would be blown apart. Israel declared itself to be in a state of war, but frantic diplomacy by the Allies managed to dissuade Israel from taking immediate punitive action. Batteries of Patriot ground-to-air missiles were dispatched to Tel Aviv, Jerusalem and Haifa. The Allies diverted 30% of their air effort to Scud hunting. But in the expanses of vast Iraqi desert all too often the air strike arrived to find the Scud fired and the mobile launcher elusively camouflaged. Previously, the US military had believed that its hi-tec satellite observation system could detect Scuds before launch. Now it was finding that the Scuds could be many minutes into flight before being betrayed by the flare from their motors. Asked by the media on 19 January about the Scud menace, the normally upbeat Schwarzkopf was obliged to say that "the picture is unclear", and to grumble that looking for Scuds was like looking for the proverbial needle in the haystack.

If the C-in-C was unclear about what to do, the Scud factor gave 22 SAS an absolutely clear-cut mission. De la Billiere signalled 22 SAS that "all SAS effort should be directed against Scuds". That very same day, 19 January, the SAS was rushed 1500 km from its holding area to an FOB just inside the Saudi border with Western Iraq. The move was made in a non-stop 24 hour airlift by the RAF Special Forces flight.

The Regiment decided on two principal means of dealing with the Scud menace. It would insert into Iraq covert

8-man static patrols to watch Main Supply Routes (MSRs) and report on the movement of Scud traffic. There would be three such patrols, South, Central and North. When Scud sites and launchers were identified, US F15 and A10 airstrikes would be called down to destroy them, directed to the target by the SAS patrol using a tactical airlink. (Though the SAS patrols carried laser-designators to "paint" targets for Allied aircraft they only used them infrequently.)

Alongside the road watch patrols, there were four columns of heavily armed vehicles, "Pink Panther" Land Rovers and Unimogs, which would penetrate the "Scud Box", an area of western desert near the border with Jordan which was thought to contain around 14 mobile launchers.

As is traditional in the SAS, the decision how to deploy was left to the patrol commanders and reached after democratic discussion.

The South and Central road watch teams were inserted on 21 January, and both found that the eerily flat, feature-less desert offered no possibility of concealment. The South road watch patrol aborted their mission and flew back on their insertion helicopter. The Central team also decided that the terrain was lethal, but before "bugging out" in their Land Rovers and stripped-down motorcycles called down an air strike on two Iraqi radars. After a four-night drive through 140 miles of bitingly cold desert the patrol reached Saudi Arabia. Four men needed treatment for frostbite.

Road Watch North, codenamed "Bravo Two Zero", had the most isolated insertion, landed by RAF Chinook 100 miles north-west of Baghdad. The weather was appalling, driving wind and sleet, the worst winter in this part of the Iraqi desert for thirty years. Led by Sgt Andy McNab (a pseudonym), the patrol took food and water for 14 days, explosives and ammunition for their 203s (American M16 rifles with 40mm grenade-launchers attached), Minimi machine guns, grenades, extra clothes, maps, compasses and survival equipment. Each man was carrying 209 lbs of kit. Watching a main supply route, the patrol saw a Scud launch and prepared to send their first situation report ("Sit Rep") to base. In the first of several fruitless efforts, Bravo Two Zero's signaller, Trooper Steven ("Legs") Lane prepared the radio antenna, encoded Sgt McNab's message and typed it ready for transmission. There was no answer and no amount of adjusting the set got a response.

On the second day an Iraqi military convoy rumbled across the desert towards the team and sited a battery of low-level anti-aircraft guns only yards from where they were hunkered down. The team got off a brief radio message to HQ: "Enemy triple-A gun now in position immediately to our north". The team was now in grave danger of compromise. In mid afternoon the compromise came. A young Iraqi goatherd looked down into the patrol's lying-up place (LUP), a shallow wadi, saw the troopers and ran off towards the Iraqi soldiers. Bravo Two Zero rapidly prepared to move, checking equipment and gulping down as much water as possible. They had a "fearsome tab" (march) in front of them.

There were further frantic efforts to radio base that they were now compromised and requested "exfil asap". There was again no response. The HF radio was being rendered near useless by ionospheric distortion. The men loaded their bergens and moved quickly westwards. As they cleared the bottom of the wadi they heard tracked vehicles approaching from the rear. They dropped into a depression and turned to face the enemy. An Iraqi Armoured Personnel Carrier (APC) opened fire with a 7.62 machine gun. With a scream of "Fucking let's do it!", the SAS patrol fired off a fusillade of 66 anti-armour rockets, rifle grenades and Minimis. They held off the Iraqis twice, destroying armoured personnel carriers and infantry trucks, and cut down scores of troops.

It started to get dark, and the patrol decided to get out of the contact area, moving as fast as they physically could manage with their heavy bergens. As they cleared a slope the Iraqi Triple-A battery sighted them and opened fire. A 57 mm ack-ack round hit one trooper in the back, ripping open his bergen. When extracted from it he was found to be uninjured. The rest of the patrol voted to "bin" their bergens for more speed, and eventually lost their enemy in the gloom. At a rallying point, Sgt McNab decided to use their four personal short-range TACBE (personal rescue beacons) to get in touch with an orbiting AWACS plane to bring strike aircraft down on the Iraqis. Again there was no reply. McNab did a quick appreciation of their situation. The Iraqis would expect them to make south for Saudi Arabia. Jordan was due West but was a non-combatant ally of Saddam Hussein. A hundred and twenty kilometres to the north west was Syria, a member of the anti-Saddam coalition. McNab decided to go for Syria.

Moving fast towards the Syrian border, Bravo Two Zero walked 50 miles that night, through driving sleet, pausing to rest only four times. Two troopers were in a parlous state, however. Sgt Vince Phillips had fractured a leg in the contact with the Iraqis and was finding it difficult to move. Trooper "Stan" was becoming dangerously dehydrated.

The sound of aircraft high overhead prompted another call on the TACBE. Finally, they got a response. An American pilot on a bombing mission acknowledged their call. The message was relayed to the British Special Ops HQ in Saudi Arabia. British and American helicopters went into Iraq to search for the patrol, but a specific run to a pre-arranged rendezvous was ruled out as too dangerous.

The stop to use the TACBE proved unlucky. In the swirling, raining darkness, Sgt Phillips, Cpl "Chris" and Trooper Stan carried on walking and became separated from the rest of the patrol.

Sgt McNab and his four companions had no option but to continue on without them, hoping they would meet up later. The rain turned to snow. During rests they huddled together for warmth. In their soaked clothes the wind-chill was starting to kill them. Throughout the night they slowly made their way to the Syrian border. Resting during the next day they decided that, if they were going to make it, they would need to hi-jack a vehicle, preferably something inconspicuous. Watching by a main road they ignored military trucks. In the gathering darkness of evening they spotted the lights of a single vehicle and flagged it down. The incident has already entered Regiment folklore. Instead of the hoped for 4WD, they found before them a bright yellow New York taxi, proudly sporting chrome bumpers and whitewall tyres. The five SAS men pulled out its amazed occupants and hopped in, putting the heater on high. They made good progress towards the border, their shamags pulled up around their faces to conceal their Caucasian identity, until they became confused in the lacework of roads near the border. Along with other traffic they were stopped by Iraqi soldiers at a vehicle checkpoint. An Iraqi "jundie" (squaddie) knocked on the driver's window to ask for their papers. Trooper Legs Lane shot the Iraqi in the head with his 203. The SAS men leaped out, shot two more soldiers and ran off into the desert.

By now the lights of a town across the border were clearly visible. As they neared the border they again ran into an anti-aircraft battery. Shells and small arms fire landed all around. There were now over 1500 Iraqi troops looking for them. The SAS men had barely six miles to go, but the moon was bright. An Iraqi patrol found them hiding in a ditch. A running firefight broke out in which the SAS soldiers killed scores of Iraqis, but became separated from each other in the process. Trooper "Mark" was wounded in the elbow and ankle and captured. Another Trooper, Robert Consiglio, a Swiss-born former Royal Marine, was hit in the head as he covered the withdrawal of Trooper "Dinger" and Lance-Corporal Lane. Consiglio was the first SAS soldier of the campaign to die from enemy fire. He received a posthumous Military Medal. Lane urged "Dinger" to join him and swim the Euphrates, then in full icy flood. Lane emerged on the far bank in a state of collapse. His companion stayed with him and hid him in a nearby hut. When it became clear that Lane was going to die from hypothermia, "Dinger" attracted the attention of a civilian working nearby. By the time an Iraqi retrieval team got to Lane he was dead. He, too, was awarded a posthumous MM. "Dinger" tried to escape but was captured.

Sergeant McNab was discovered the next morning in a drainage culvert. Along with the other SAS men captured alive he suffered a month of imprisonment and torture. The latter was brutally physical and, ultimately, counter-productive. It only made the SAS men more determined not to talk. Though the Iraqi military imprisoned the men together they failed to even covertly monitor their conversations.

As for the trio missing in the desert, Sergeant Phillips was lost in driving snow on the night of 26 January. His companions, "Stan" and "Chris" turned back for him but could not find him. His body was eventually found by Iraqi soldiers and handed to the British authorities at the war's end. Later the next day, Stan went to see if he could hi-jack some transport. As he approached a parked lorry an Iraqi soldier came out of the house. The Iraqi tried to pull a weapon out. Stan shot him with his 203. Six or seven other Iraqi soldiers came running out. Stan shot three of them but then his gun jammed. The Iraqis did not kill him, only beat him unconscious with their rifle butts. When Stan failed to return to the LUP, Chris decided to set out on his own. He would be the only man from Bravo Two Zero to escape to safety.

Massively dehydrated, his feet and hands turning septic from cuts, and at one point falling unconscious and breaking his nose, Chris managed to cross the Syrian border on 30 January. He had covered 117 miles, evading hundreds of Iraqi searchers, with only two packets of biscuits for nourishment. During the final two days he was without any water. He had filled his bottles from a small stream. When he came to drink the water his lips and mouth burned instantly. The stream was polluted with chemicals from a nearby uranium processing plant.

Inside Syria, Chris was initially treated with hostility. As he neared the capital Damascus, however, his treatment became more cordial. A civilian pin-stripe suit was run up for him as he bathed in the HQ of the Syrian secret police. That same night he was handed over to the British Embassy. It was the first anyone at SAS HQ in Saudi Arabia had heard of Bravo Two Zero since infiltration. The seven day walk of Trooper Chris across the desert is considered by the Regiment to be at least equal to that of Jack Sillitoe, an SAS "Original", who crossed the North African desert in 1942 drinking his own urine to survive. In a Regiment where the remarkable is standard, Chris's epic trek is still considered one of the most amazing escapades ever recorded.

The eight members of Road Watch North, Bravo Two Zero, killed nearly 250 Iraqis in their fight and flight across northern Iraq. After the attempt to insert the static patrols, 22 SAS effort shifted to the four mobile fighting columns. Drawn from Squadrons A and D, the columns — which contained about a dozen Land Rovers or Unimogs together with motorcycle out-riders — were the biggest overland fighting force put into the field by the SAS since 1945. The columns had their own Stinger anti-aircraft and Milan anti-tank missiles, plus .5 Browning machine guns, 7.62 mm general purpose machine guns and 40 mm grenade launchers. One team found a sledge-hammer most useful. The freebooting columns, soon operating in broad daylight, scored spectacular successes as they sped into the Iraqi desert flying enormous Union flags to identify them to friendly aircraft. An Iraqi deputy commander of a gun battery taken POW proved to have on his person a map giving positions of Iraqi front lines

*units. On 29 January SAS columns called down F15E airstrikes
on two mobile Scud launchers, plus one fixed site. On 3 February
in the Wadi Amij ("Scud Alley") locality, a patrol from D
Squadron called down an airstrike on a Scud convoy. Only one
airstrike hit the target, so the SAS patrol hit the convoy with
wire-guided Milan anti-tank missiles, an inspired last minute
addition to the SAS armoury. These SAS attacks were the first
military actions on the ground in the war except for the minor
Iraqi cross-border attack on Khafji, Saudi Arabia, on 29 January.
Group 2 from D Squadron called an airstrike on a Scud convoy
on 5 February, and on the same day fought two firefights with
Iraqi troops. Increasingly, the SAS destroyed Scud and launcher
themselves, since some were escaping in the gap between their
targetting by the SAS and the arrival of the airstrike. To service
the Land Rovers and Unimogs, the SAS organised a supply
column ("E Squadron") which formed a temporary workshop
deep inside Iraq. Everywhere the SAS teams went they caused
mayhem, and not only to the Scuds. Saddam (courtesy of the time
when the West regarded him as a friend) had an advanced
communications network consisting of buried fibre optic cables.
The weak point in the system was that the signal needed to be
boosted at above-ground relay stations. A team from 22 SAS
blew up seven of these stations alongside the highway from
Baghdad to Amman. When the SAS Land Rovers returned to
Saudi Arabia at the end of the war, they had covered an average
of 1500 miles and spent between 36 and 42 days behind the lines.
The front wings of the Land Rovers were decorated with scores of
silhouettes of "kills", including mobile scuds and communications
towers. The SAS had also provided valuable advice to US Special
Forces, operating in a "Scud Box" north of the Regiment's. It is a
measure of the success of the SAS that General Norman
Schwarzkopf, the "enemy" of special forces, praised the Regiment's "totally outstanding performance" in the Gulf. (See
Appendix C for the full text of Schwarzkopf's letter of commen-
dation for 22 SAS.) No less than 39 awards and honours for
bravery and meritorious service were given the Regiment for its*

part in Operation Granby, the Gulf War. There was, of course, a price to be paid for the Regiment's achievement. In addition to the three SAS soldiers from Bravo Two Zero who were killed, Trooper David Denbury from A Squadron was killed on 21 February during the ambush of a Scud convoy in North-West Iraq. A sapper attached to the Regiment was also killed in action.

Chapter Nine

BIRTH OF A LEGEND

Jon E. Lewis

M *ost of the North African campaign of 1940–43 was*
fought out in the narrow coastal strip which runs the long
arc from Tunis to Cairo. South of the coastal strip lies the
Sahara, an immense secret place of shifting sands and cauldron-
like heat. Few paid much attention to this wilderness, but in its
unguarded vastness a young British second-lieutenant saw the
possibility for a new type of unit to operate. A unit which would
strike swift and hard, and then disappear like a phantom into the
desert from which it had emerged.

The Special Air Service was conceived in a hospital bed in
Egypt. Injured during some unofficial parachute training
David Stirling, a subaltern with No. 8 (Guards) Commando,
decided to use his enforced stay in the Alexandria Scottish
Military Hospital to develop a scheme for special opera-
tions in the desert.

On his release from hospital in July 1941, Stirling
determined to bring his plan to the attention of the
Commander-in-Chief. As C-in-Cs are not, by and large,
in the habit of granting interviews to junior officers Stirling
decided to ignore the usual channels. Instead, he hobbled on
his crutches to British Army Middle East HQ and tricked his
way past the sentry. Inside, Stirling found his way into the
office of the Deputy Commander Middle East, one General
Neil Ritchie. Stirling apologised to the somewhat surprised
Ritchie for the unconventional call, but insisted that he had
something of "great operational importance" to tell him.

Ritchie offered him a seat, and Stirling pulled out the pencilled memo on a desert raiding force he had prepared in hospital.

Ritchie spent several minutes reading it. It was then Stirling's turn to be surprised. Ritchie looked up and said brusquely, "I think this may be the sort of plan we are looking for. I will discuss it with the Commander-in-Chief and let you know our decision in the next day or so." The C-in-C was General Auckinleck, new to his command and under pressure from Churchill to mount an offensive. Stirling's plan was indeed what Auckinleck was looking for. It required few resources, and it was original. The unit Stirling proposed was to operate behind enemy lines in order to attack vulnerable targets like extended supply lines and airfields. What is more, the raids were to be carried out by very small groups of men, between five and ten, rather than the standard commando force of hundreds.

Meanwhile, Ritchie looked into Stirling's background. He was pleased with what he found. David Stirling, born in 1915, was the youngest son of the aristocratic Brigadier Archibald Stirling of Keir. After three years at Cambridge, David Stirling had joined the Scots Guards, before transferring to No. 8 Commando. As part of the "Layforce" brigade, No. 8 had been dispatched to North Africa where its seaborne raids had all proved to be wash outs. The unit, along with the rest of Layforce, had been marked for disbandment. Stirling, however, had remained so keen on the commando idea that he had jumped – literally – at the chance of doing some parachuting with 'chutes that another officer in No. 8, Jock Lewes, had scrounged. The jumping trials had taken place near Mersa Matruh. The aircraft used, a lumbering Valentia bi-plane, was not equipped for parachuting and the men had secured the static lines which open the parachutes to seat legs. Stirling's parachute had caught on the door and snagged. He had descended far too rapidly and damaged his back badly on landing. Which is how he had come to be in Alexandria Hospital.

Three days after his meeting with Ritchie, Stirling was back at Middle East HQ, this time with a pass. Auckinleck saw him in person. Stirling was given permission to recruit a force of six other officers and sixty men. The unit was to be called "L Detachment, SAS Brigade". The SAS stood for Special Air Service, which did not exist. The name was dreamed up by Brigadier Dudley Clarke, a staff Intelligence Officer, as a means of convincing the enemy that the British possessed a large airborne force in North Africa. To mark his new appointment, Stirling was promoted to captain.

The recruiting took less than a week. There were two particular officers Stirling wanted. The first was Jock Lewes who was in Tobruk, where he had been carrying out small raids against enemy outposts. A scholar and Oxford rowing "blue", Lewes was also a daring soldier. He agreed to join. So did the Northern Irishman Paddy Mayne, then under close arrest for striking his commanding officer. Before the war, Mayne had been a rugby player of international rank. Most of the rest of the unit were recruited from the Guards Commando then at a camp at Genefa. Selection was based on Stirling's impression of the men at brief interviews. He also told them that if they failed to make the grade in training they would have to return to their units.

By August 1941, Stirling had established his force at Kabrit, 100 miles south of Cairo. Equipment was conspicuous by its absence. The camp consisted of two small tents for personnel, one large supply tent and a wooden sign saying "L Detachment – S.A.S.". Being, in his own words a "cheekie laddie", Stirling decided that the equipment L Detachment needed, in view of the parsimony of the Q side, would have to be "borrowed" from a New Zealand camp down the road. Thus the first – and highly unofficial – mission of L Detachment was a night raid on the New

Zealand camp, filling L Detachment's one and only 3-ton truck with anything useful that could be found.

The next day, L Detachment boasted the smartest – and most luxuriously furnished – British camp in the Canal Zone. Training then began in earnest. From the start, Stirling insisted on a high standard of discipline – equal to that of the Brigade of Guards – and the pursuit of excellence. To achieve such standards demanded a combination of the right character and sheer physical fitness. One early recruit to Stirling's L Detachment, Fitzroy Maclean, recalled that: "for days and nights on end, we trudged interminably over the alternating soft sand and jagged rocks of the desert, weighed down by heavy loads of explosive, eating and drinking only what we could carry with us. In the intervals we did weapon training, physical training and training in demolitions and navigation."

Additionally, everyone joining the SAS had to be a parachutist, since Stirling envisaged airborne insertions for his force. No RAF instructors – or indeed aircraft – were available, so the SAS developed its own parachute training techniques. These involved jumping from ever higher platforms or from the backs of trucks moving at 30mph. The unit then moved on to make its first live jump, from a Bombay aircraft. Two men died when their 'chutes failed to open. "That night", recalled SAS "Original" Bob Bennett, "we went to bed with as many cigarettes as possible and smoked until morning. Next day, every man (led by Stirling himself) jumped; no-one backed out. It was then that I realised that I was with a great bunch of chaps." Thereafter parachute training progressed smoothly.

There were other problems though. Prime among them was the type of bomb which would be carried by the SAS raiding parties; it had to be small enough to be easily transportable but big enough to do the job. The requisite device was invented by Jock Lewes, a small incendiary bomb made of oil, plastic and thermite. Appropriately enough, it became known as the Lewes bomb.

Stirling sharpened his men for action with a training raid on the large RAF base at Heliopolis outside Cairo. An RAF Group-Captain had been unwise enough to tell L Detachment that their planned enterprise of attacking enemy aircraft on the ground was unrealistic. Although the airfield guards had been warned of their coming, and daily reconnaissance planes sent up, the SAS could not be kept out. After marching 90 miles across desert by night and hiding up by day, they placed stickers representing bombs on the RAF aircraft before slipping away into the desert darkness.

To celebrate their success, L Detachment were given a few days leave in Cairo. Before they had lacked an identity, but training had made them into a cohesive unit. They took pride, too, in their new unit insignia. The design of the cap badge was the result of a competition won by Sergeant Bob Tait who came up with a winged dagger emblem. David Stirling added the motto, "Who Dares Wins". The one problem was the unit's headgear: a white beret. After this drew unceremonious wolf whistles in Cairo, it was hurriedly replaced, first by a khaki forage cap, then by the famous sand-coloured beret.

After their leave, the men of L Detachment assembled to hear the details of their first real attack, scheduled for the night of 17 November 1941, when five SAS groups would parachute into the desert near Gazala and attack the five forward German fighter airfields. It was to be the opening prelude to Auckinleck's attempt to relieve Tobruk. Stirling assembled his men. "With luck", he told them, "we'll polish off Rommel's entire fighter force." There were whistles and cheers.

Alas, L Detachment's luck was out.

The weather forecast on the morning of 16 November looked ominous. The wind was strong and it looked as though it might rain — far from ideal conditions for parachuting. Even so, Stirling decided to press ahead with the mission, partly because Auckinleck expected it, mostly because many of the men who had joined the SAS had done so out of disgust for the continual cancellation of their commando operations. To call off the drop, Stirling concluded, would have been catastrophic for morale. At 19.30 the five Bombays containing L Detachment left the runway, flying first out to sea, then turning inland to cross the coast well behind German lines. The aircraft tossed around wildly in the wind, and the ground below was totally obscured by the darkness and the sandstorm.

The drop was more than a failure, it was a disaster. Of his group, Stirling was the first to jump. It was so black and murky that he could not see the ground. He waited and waited for the impact. He recorded later that it was like being suspended in space. Then there was a smashing blow. For some seconds he was unconscious but luckily nothing was broken. It took him nearly an hour to assemble the rest of his stick who had been dragged all over the desert by the wind. One man could not be found, others were injured, and vital supplies were missing. They had some Lewes bombs, but no detonators and so could not carry out their mission. Stirling resolved on the spot that never again would detonators and bombs be packed separately. There was nothing to do but call off the attack and attempt to walk the forty miles into the desert for the planned rendezvous with a motor patrol from the Long Range Desert Group (LRDG).

It took several days for the SAS parties to reach the LRDG rendezvous. Some never made it. Of the fifty one officers and men who had jumped into the storm three days before, only five officers (including Stirling himself) and eighteen men were left. Any other man would have given up the idea of a special desert force.

Stirling, however, decided to press ahead. Fortunately for him, the Eighth Army Command had more to think about than the fortunes of a small band of irregulars; the counteroffensive against Rommel had become bogged down by tough German resistance. So Stirling withdrew with the remnants of his unit to a remote oasis at Gialo, where he began preparing for another mission. He had already abandoned the idea of parachuting into the desert. At the rendezvous with the LRDG, David Lloyd-Owen of the latter unit had proposed that his patrols could get Stirling and his men to and from their targets. Although essentially a reconnaissance group, such a task was easily within the LRDG's capability. Stirling accepted with alacrity. Now, at Gialo, Stirling and his men poured over maps. A quick success was obviously necessary to wipe out the failure of the first raid, if hostile elements at GQ were not to succeed in burying the fledgling SAS.

In only a matter of days Stirling's idea was vindicated. In early December an SAS group under Paddy Mayne destroyed 24 enemy aircraft at Tamet airfield, while Bill Fraser's party destroyed 37 at Agedabia. Two weeks later, Paddy Mayne led a six-man group back to Tamet and accounted for a further 27 aircraft. A group led by Stirling himself reached the airfield at Bagush but were unable to plant their bombs. Their improvised response to this situation was to prove so successful that it was used often in future: a motorised charge down the airstrip, blazing away at the aircraft with machine guns and grenades from the back of the LRDG jeeps.

Fitzroy Maclean later wrote of the huge success of these raids:

"Working on these lines, David achieved a series of successes which surpassed the wildest expectations of those who had originally supported his venture. No sooner had the enemy become aware of his presence in one part of the desert then he was attacking them somewhere else. Never has the element of surprise, the key to success in all irregular warfare, been more brilliantly exploited. Soon the number of aircraft destroyed was well into three figures."

It was not only aircraft which received the attention of the SAS. Stirling was quick to see the vulnerability of Rommel's Supply lines. Convoys were attacked, harbours raided. Recruits flocked to join L Detachment. Stirling himself was promoted to Major in January 1942. Seven months later, Stirling's force had grown to Regimental size (750 men) and was renamed 1 SAS.

Perhaps the real proof of the SAS concept was that it survived without the presence of its founder, it wasn't dependent on the charisma and drive of one man. David Stirling led from the front and in January 1943 he paid the price. He was captured in Tunisia by the Germans. The SAS went on without him, not only in North Africa, but into Italy, France, Holland and eventually Germany. By 1945, the idea David Stirling had conceived in his hospital bed had become more than a war-winning unit. It had become a legend.